lonely planet

# Diving & Snorkeling

# Honduras'
# Bay Islands

David Behrens

Cam O'Brien

LONELY PLANET PUBLICATIONS
Melbourne • Oakland • London • Paris

**Diving & Snorkeling Honduras' Bay Islands**
- A Lonely Planet Pisces Book

**1st Edition – March 2002**

**Published by**
**Lonely Planet Publications Pty Ltd,** ABN 36 005 607 983
90 Maribyrnong St., Footscray, Victoria 3011, Australia

**Other offices**
150 Linden Street, Oakland, California 94607, USA
10a Spring Place, London NW5 3BH, UK

**Photographs**
by photographers as indicated

**Front cover photograph**
by Michael Lawrence
Marine life along one of the Bay Islands' spectacular walls

**Back cover photographs**
Dolphin and friend at Anthony's Key Resort,
by Steve  Rosenberg
Brittle star rests atop vase sponge, by David Behrens
Roátan reef, by Michael Lawrence

All of the images in this guide are available for
   licensing from **Lonely Planet Images**
www.lonelyplanetimages.com

ISBN 1 74059 058 9

text & maps © Lonely Planet Publications Pty Ltd 2002
photographs © photographers as indicated 2002
dive site maps are Transverse Mercator projection

Lonely Planet, the Lonely Planet logo, Lonely Planet Images,
CitySync and eKno are trademarks of Lonely Planet Publications Pty Ltd.
Other trademarks are the property of their respective owners.

Printed by HingYip Printing Ltd., China

# Contents

# Authors

## David Behrens

A practicing marine biologist since 1974, David Behrens has authored three marine life identification guides and more than 70 technical and popular papers about marine life and ecology and related topics. He holds a master's degree in marine biology from San Francisco State University and is a research associate with the California Academy of Sciences. Dave and his wife, Diana, operate Sea Challengers Natural History Books, Etc. (www.seachallengers.com), a marine life and natural history book business. Dave was drawn to the Bay Islands in 1998, when he initiated a reef ecology education program on Roatán with help from Cam and Ted O'Brien, owners of the Bay Islands Beach Resort.

## Cam O'Brien

Cam O'Brien and her family first visited the Bay Islands in 1982. In 1994 Cam and her husband, Ted, left executive jobs in the U.S., bought the Bay Islands Beach Resort on Roatán and became residents of Honduras. With help from her staff, she's since built a historic village re-creation that captures the Bay Islands' social and economic past from AD 400 to 1860, compiled *Roatán's Old Timers' Cookbook* and opened Mr. Otis' Bush Medicine Garden. Cam's fascination with reefs and their critical role in island life led her to author *Islands, Reefs & Islanders: A Layman's Training Guide to the Growth & Survival of Reefs*.

## From the Authors

We would like to thank the following people for their help and willingness to share their love of the Bay Islands: the Raymond family of Sandy Bay; the staff, divemasters and guests at Bay Islands Beach Resort; Linda Fouke at Guanaja's Bayman Bay Club; Arlene White and Liz Wayne at Utila's Laguna Beach Resort; the mayors of Roatán, Jerry Hynds and Arlie Thompson, and their staff; and other resort owners throughout the islands. Special thanks to Doc Radowski, Yuval Erlich and Tim O'Leary for their expertise and assistance.

Dave Behrens would especially like to thank his wife, Diana, for her generous support during the project, his son, Michael, who assisted in Roatán, and daughters Samantha and Christy, for keeping dad honest.

Cam O'Brien sends eternal gratitude to her husband, Ted, daughter Cathy, and daughter and son-in-law Patti and Bob Beaumont, whose strength, opinions and challenges brought her to this special island and its people.

## Photography Notes

Underwater, Dave Behrens uses a Nikonos V, with Sea & Sea YS-30, YS-60 and YS-120 strobes, a 35mm lens and various extension tubes for macrophotography. He prefers Fujichrome Velvia 50 and Kodachrome 64 slide films.

## Contributing Photographers

Dave Behrens took most of the photographs in this book. Thanks also to Michael Lawrence, Steve Rosenberg, Laura Losito, Juha Tamminen, Graeme Teague, Michael Behrens, Scott Tuason, Michael McKay and Greg Johnston for their photo contributions.

## From the Publisher

This first edition was published in Lonely Planet's U.S. office under the guidance of Roslyn Bullas, the Pisces Books publishing manager. David Lauterborn edited the text and photos with invaluable help from Roslyn Bullas and buddy checks from Sarah Hubbard and Michael Johnson. Emily Douglas designed the cover and Gerilyn Attebery designed the interior with assistance from Emily. Navigating the nautical charts was cartographer Brad Lodge, who created the maps, with assistance from Sara Nelson and Rachel Driver. U.S. cartography manager Alex Guilbert supervised map production.

## Pisces Pre-Dive Safety Guidelines

Before embarking on a scuba diving, skin diving or snorkeling trip, carefully consider the following to help ensure a safe and enjoyable experience:

- Possess a current diving certification card from a recognized scuba diving instructional agency (if scuba diving)
- Be sure you are healthy and feel comfortable diving
- Obtain reliable information about physical and environmental conditions at the dive site (e.g., from a reputable local dive operation)
- Be aware of local laws, regulations and etiquette about marine life and environment
- Dive at sites within your experience level; if possible, engage the services of a competent, professionally trained dive instructor or divemaster

Underwater conditions vary significantly from one region, or even site, to another. Seasonal changes can significantly alter site and dive conditions. These differences influence the way divers dress for a dive and what diving techniques they use.

There are special requirements for diving in any area, regardless of location. Before your dive, ask about environmental characteristics that can affect your diving and how trained local divers deal with these considerations.

## Warning & Request

Things change—dive site conditions, regulations, topside information. Nothing stays the same for long. Your feedback on this book will be used to help update and improve the next edition. Excerpts from your correspondence may appear in *Planet Talk*, our quarterly newsletter, or *Comet*, our monthly email newsletter. Please let us know if you do not want your letter published or your name acknowledged.

Correspondence can be addressed to:
**Lonely Planet Publications**
**Pisces Books**
150 Linden Street
Oakland, CA 94607
email: pisces@lonelyplanet.com

# Introduction

With smiles as warm as the Caribbean sunshine, Bay Islanders welcome visitors to a world of pristine coral reefs and panoramic vistas. Lush green hills abound with flowers and fruit and are home to colorful birds and butterflies, deer, rabbits, iguanas and other fauna. Roatán, Barbareta, Guanaja and Utila are the largest of the 67 islands and cays, and the Cayos Cochinos lie halfway between Utila and mainland Honduras. Originally a destination solely for divers, the islands now offer land-based activities for divers and nondivers alike.

DAVID BEHRENS

Outside the resorts you won't find the crowds, beachside peddlers, rows of duty-free shops, casinos, high-rises or other signs of modern life now changing many Caribbean getaways. What you will find are local parties in tiny beach bars, rustic shops with handmade crafts and an easygoing pace that soothes the soul. Dense jungle growth competes with narrow winding roads to reclaim the land. Islanders on horseback share the roads with crowded, dilapidated cabs. Simple

houses of wood and reeds mix with more upscale homes. The aroma of smoldering brush fires is present each morning, as smoke spirals down the coastal slopes. The term "island time" may have been invented here.

The Bay Islands' reefs support 99% of the hard coral, gorgonian and sponge species and 100% of the fish species found in the Caribbean. Divers and snorkelers cruise the reef with rays, turtles, sharks and eels and search crevices for octopuses, nudibranchs, lobsters, crabs and conchs. Whale shark sightings are not unusual, and snorkeling alongside these huge peaceful creatures is an unforgettable experience. While the calm, warm waters are perfect for the beginning diver, the variety of dive sites—including spur-and-groove formations, swim-throughs, tunnels, caves, walls, reef crests and wrecks—satisfies even the most advanced diver. Many moored dive sites crest in 30ft (9m) of water, allowing snorkelers easy access to the reeftop.

This guide describes dive sites off **Roatán**, **Barbareta**, **Guanaja**, the **Cayos Cochinos** and **Utila**. You'll find specific information on 74 of the best sites in the Bay Islands, including location, depth, access and recommended diving expertise. You'll also learn about each site's underwater topography and the marine life you may encounter. The Marine Life section offers a peek at the Bay Islands' most common vertebrates and invertebrates. While the book is not intended as a stand-alone travel guide, the Overview and Practicalities sections provide useful information about the region, and the Activities & Attractions section offers suggestions for nondiving days.

Best friends stand beside a traditional wooden dugout fishing boat, or *cayuco*.

# Overview

The Bay Islands are geographically and culturally distinct from the rest of Central America. Just off the north coast of Honduras, Roatán, Barbareta, Guanaja, Utila and the Cayos Cochinos are literally the terrestrial peaks of the submarine Bonacca Ridge. This region's colorful history is reflected in the faces of its highly diverse population, including people of African, Afro-Carib (Garífuna), mestizo and Spanish descent, as well as recent émigrés from Europe and the Americas.

MICHAEL LAWRENCE

About 30 miles (50km) long and no more than 2¹/₂ miles (4km) wide, Roatán is the largest of the island group. Its 16,000-plus population is concentrated in some half dozen settlements and a number of ethnically homogeneous enclaves. Off its eastern tip is Barbareta, a 1,200-acre privately owned wildlife refuge.

Boasting thickly forested slopes and no paved roads, mountainous Guanaja (referred to as the Isle of Pines by Christopher Columbus) is the second largest island. Although the main island is 21 sq miles (54 sq km) in area, most of its nearly 6,000 inhabitants live in the overwater settlement of Bonacca, on a small offshore cay.

The Cayos Cochinos offer views of unspoiled tropical beauty.

**11**

The smallest of the major islands is Utila (population 2,000), known among the international backpacker set for its dive bargains. Pumpkin Hill is the only ripple in its otherwise flat 16 sq mile (41 sq km) landscape.

Equidistant from Utila and the mainland are the Cayos Cochinos. Collectively designated a biological marine reserve, this unspoiled island group is home to a handful of private owners.

The Bay Islands' principal renewable resource is the coral reef ecosystem, which provides islanders with both food and a tourism draw. To protect this precious resource, islanders and resort operators now work together to protect and manage the environment, promote sustainable development and boost conservation and habitat restoration efforts.

## Hurricane Mitch

In 1998 Hurricane Mitch roared into the Gulf of Honduras. Packing winds up to 180mph, this devastating storm lashed the islands for five days. Though Mitch defoliated much of Guanaja and scoured Punta Gorda and Oak Ridge on Roatán, the islands largely escaped disaster. Resort owners cleaned the beaches and rebuilt their docks, and most were open for business within two weeks. Unfortunately, the Honduras mainland was devastated, and journalists reported to the world that all of Honduras—including the islands—had been decimated. Tourism dried up overnight, spelling economic disaster for the islands and their people.

At this writing, the tourism industry is just recovering. Guanaja's mangroves and Caribbean pines are growing back, Punta Gorda is almost completely rebuilt and the reefs have never looked so good.

Hurricanes are seasonal occurrences in the Caribbean, and warnings precede the storms by several days. While islanders are used to these periodic storms and know how to weather them, you'll have ample time to change your travel plans if you desire.

Mitch left beaches eroded and trees stripped of foliage.

# Geography

The Western Caribbean reaches from the Yucatán Peninsula in the north, south past the Belize Barrier Reef, then eastward along Honduras' north coast. The Bay Islands are tucked into this L-shaped area, about 30 miles (50 km) offshore. Bordering the mainland to the west and south are Guatemala, Nicaragua, El Salvador and the Pacific Ocean.

# Geology

Extending deep beneath the sea, the Bonacca Ridge parallels the Honduras mainland to the south and the Bartlett Trough to the north. Over millions of years, plate tectonics, earthquakes and volcanic action have given rise to the chain now known as the Bay Islands. Underwater, the geologic upheaval has left behind a range of interesting dive sites, from steep walls and spur-and-groove reefs to swim-throughs, tunnels and caves. At the peak of the last ice age, some 18,000 years ago, the islands' reefs were exposed, and divers can still find evidence of freshwater streams, springs and even an ancient waterfall now below sea level.

## What Is Ironshore?

The jagged black shoreline formation Bay Islanders call "ironshore" is actually elevated fossil coral reef dating back more than a million years to the Pleistocene epoch. This limestone composition is more commonly known as karst.

DAVID BEHRENS

Rising to 771ft (235m), a lush green mountain ridge runs down the center of Roatán. The shoreline features scattered beaches and limestone outcrops. Clinging to its east end are the smaller islands of Helena, Morat and Barbareta. At 300ft (90m), Utila is the lowest island, with a shoreline similar to that of Roatán. Guanaja's shoreline is composed of large shale slabs. You'll also find the steepest terrain and highest altitude (1,342ft, or 409m). The Cayos Cochinos comprise several small sandy cays and two larger, heavily vegetated islands with rocky shorelines. The largest of the group is Cochino Grande, which tops out at 465ft (142m).

# History

Bay Islands history is a microcosm of Caribbean history. Even today you may encounter the descendents of Indians, pirates, slavers, loggers, English sailors and soldiers, Spanish conquistadors, African slaves, freemen and Americans.

Indians inhabited the islands as far back as AD 400. Researchers are relatively certain the resident Indians were the Pech, or Paya, originally from Colombia. Conflict between Central American Indian tribes was not unusual, with warriors raiding neighboring villages for slaves, food and other bounty. On the islands life was probably not as violent, as food was readily available and populations sustainable.

Europeans first arrived on the scene in the 1500s. In 1502, on his fourth and final voyage to the New World, Christopher Columbus landed on Guanaja. Crew who went ashore reported that the Indians were "warlike archers who made a good beer and bread from a root they grew."

Columbus "recruited" a local Indian trader as an interpreter. The interpreter understood the language spoken by Indians along the north coast of what is now Honduras. However, once the party turned south and reached what's now known as Nicaragua, the natives spoke a different language and turned violent. Columbus gave that area a wide berth and sent the Indian interpreter home. Reports of these explorations opened the islands to centuries of exploration and exploitation.

In the early 1500s the Spanish governor of Cuba raided the Bay Islands for slaves, returning to Havana with more than 500 Indians. Barely in the harbor, the captives revolted, overthrew the Spaniards and sailed back home. Infuriated, the governor sent a second fleet to raid the islands, returning to Cuba with 800 Indians and leaving another 100 dead. In 1518 a third raiding party was organized, though this time the crew refused to go, saying it was against God's will to enslave men.

For a few years public sentiment turned against the slave trade, spearheaded by missionaries and Spain's Queen Isabella. But the demand for a cheap labor force and desire for new converts to Christianity soon led to the reinstitution of slavery.

From the 1500s well into the late 1700s the islands served as a way station for pirates, Spanish conquistadors and English soldiers. Deep harbors, plentiful food and easy access to trade routes between Europe and the Americas made the islands desirable to both Spain and England. In 1642, tired of English intervention, the Spanish raided the islands and moved the Indians to the north coast of Honduras. The islands were left empty.

Pirates continued to use Roatán as a haven to refurbish their ships and restock supplies, and English businessmen sent logging crews to the coasts of Belize and Honduras. Despite Spain's ownership claim to the islands, in 1742 the English again sent ships to Roatán in order to start a settlement. By 1748 they were ordered to leave and abandoned the settlement.

In 1798 the Garífuna (black Caribs from St. Vincent) were marooned on Roatán. Many migrated to the mainland, but others stayed to settle the village of Punta Gorda. This village is still inhabited by the Garífuna, and many of its inhabitants speak an African dialect.

As the political situation changed and slavery was abolished throughout the Caribbean, migrations between islands picked up. Plantation owners, freemen and former slaves from the Caymans and Belize moved to the Bay Islands.

Traditional fishing huts still line remote stretches of beach.

Widespread immigration continues today. More than 2,000 Europeans and Americans have become residents, and increasing numbers of mainland Hondurans have moved to the islands in search of better-paying jobs. Fishing, the predominant industry for years, is being usurped by tourism. Resorts, bed-and-breakfasts, dive shops, restaurants and bars are springing up to attract divers, snorkelers, ecotourists and cruise ship passengers.

The influx of tourists, foreigners and mainlanders has put additional stress on the islands' limited infrastructure. The main islands now have telephone service and varying degrees of electrical service and roads. Roatán is the most developed of the group. A paved road runs from West End to Oak Ridge, and its new airport allows direct international jet service. The World Bank is funding construction of a water and sewage-treatment system in Roatán's three major towns. Other islands have few if any paved roads, and airline service is still limited.

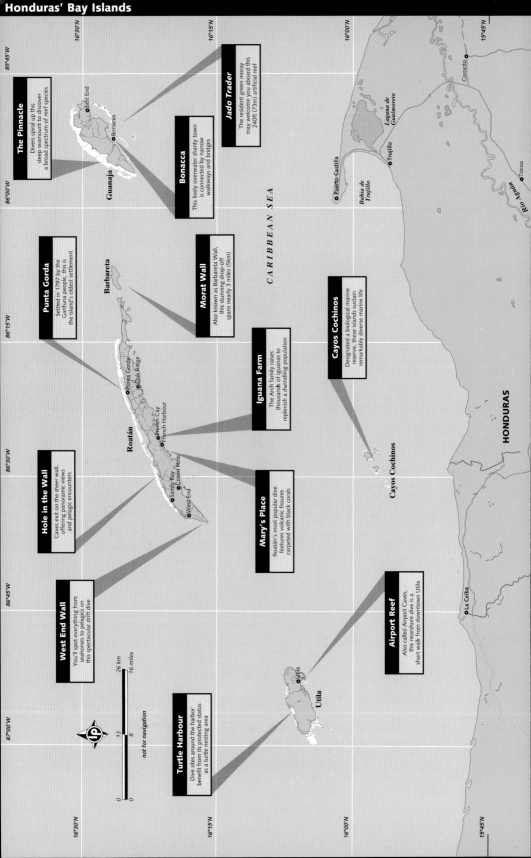

# Honduras' Bay Islands

**The Pinnacle**
Divers spiral up this steep seamount to discover a broad spectrum of reef species

**Bonacca**
This lively overwater shanty town is connected by narrow walkways and bridges

**Jado Trader**
The resident green moray may welcome you aboard this 240ft (73m) artificial reef

**Punta Gorda**
Settled in 1797 by the Garífuna people, this is the island's oldest settlement

**Morat Wall**
Also known as Barbareta Wall, this stunning drop-off spans nearly 3 miles (5km)

**Cayos Cochinos**
Designated a biological marine reserve, these islands sustain remarkably diverse marine life

**Iguana Farm**
The Arch family raises thousands of iguanas to replenish a dwindling population

**Hole in the Wall**
Caves exit on the sheer wall, offering panoramic views and pelagic encounters

**Mary's Place**
Roatán's most popular dive features volcanic fissures carpeted with black corals

**West End Wall**
You'll spot everything from seahorses to pelagics on this spectacular drift dive

**Airport Reef**
Also called Airport Caves, this nearshore dive is a short walk from downtown Utila

**Turtle Harbour**
Dive sites around the harbor benefit from its protected status as a turtle nesting area

CARIBBEAN SEA

HONDURAS

Guanaja
East End
Bonacca

Barbareta

Roatán
Punta Gorda
Oak Ridge
Helen Cay
French Harbour
Coxen Hole
Sandy Bay
West End

Cayos Cochinos

Utila
Utila

La Ceiba
Puerto Castilla
Trujillo
Bahía de Trujillo
Corocito
Tocoa
Laguna de Guaimoreto
Río Aguán

26 km
16 miles
13
8
0
0
not for navigation

# Practicalities

MICHAEL LAWRENCE

## Climate

The Bay Islands experience definite seasons. Springtime temperatures range in the 80s Fahrenheit (27 to 32°C), and the southeast trade winds blow strongly. Seas along the south shores may be rough during this period. By June the islands boast summertime temperatures up to 90°F (32°C), with steadily increasing humidity into September. Light rain showers, occasional evening thunderstorms and the ever-present trade winds help keep temperatures pleasant.

Historically, most tropical storms miss the Bay Islands, with an average of one major hurricane every 17 years. October through January is considered the rainy season, with the chance of a three-day "norther" blowing in. The normally calm, leeward north shore then becomes the rough side, and many north shore dive operators take their boats to the south shore until the wind and seas settle. Air temperatures may drop into the low 70s or upper 60s Fahrenheit (20 to 22°C) for a day or two.

Divers benefit from the islands' minimal currents and tides. Visibility is usually 80 to 120ft (24 to 37m), though it can drop due to storm runoff, coral spawning and other natural and manmade factors. Water temperatures range from 80 to 84°F (27 and 29°C) for most of the year, dropping to between 74 and 76°F (23 and 24°C) in the winter.

## Language

While Honduras' official language is Spanish, most Bay Islanders are bilingual, speaking English and Spanish with a Caribbean lilt. Dialects vary between communities. Some islanders speak with a distinct Irish/Scottish brogue, and the Garífuna in Punta Gorda still use an African dialect. Other islanders speak patois, which can be difficult to understand—politely ask them to speak slowly till you get used to the cadence. Spanish is taught in the schools, mandatory for legal documents and more prevalent in daily life.

Check island bookstores for a guide called *Wee Speak*, a fun read that defines hundreds of colloquial island expressions.

## A Fish by Any Other Name

Bay Islanders have an entirely separate vernacular for the common fish that comprise their local cuisine. The name may describe the physical characteristics of the fish (longjaw), its behavior (suckfish) or what it does to you if you come in contact with it (numbfish). Following are some examples:

| | | | |
|---|---|---|---|
| **longjaw** | barracuda | **suckfish** | remora |
| **blackapickie** | damselfish | **old shoe** | schoolmaster |
| **prukpruk** | black durgon | **numbfish** | scorpionfish |
| **squab** | parrotfish | **conchituna** | squirrelfish |
| **galambo** | large parrotfish | **woe-be-gone** | toadfish |
| **blue tumpa** | blue parrotfish | **old wife** | queen triggerfish |

# Getting There

American, Continental and TACA airlines offer daily service to Roatán through San Pedro Sula or Tegucigalpa. TACA also offers direct flights to Roatán—from New Orleans on Fridays, Houston on Saturdays and Miami on Sundays. As part of a code-sharing agreement with American, TACA has air desks in San Francisco, Los Angeles, New York, Washington, D.C., and Germany. California travelers may opt to fly through San Salvador to the island (usually with a short stop in San Pedro Sula). On each island, live-aboard operators and most dive resorts greet their guests at the airport. Occasionally, Canadian tour operators offer charters to Roatán. A few cruise ships also travel to Roatán.

DAVID BEHRENS

On the mainland, the city of La Ceiba offers daily connecting flights to the Bay Islands.

Those trying to reach the other islands have limited options. They can fly into San Pedro Sula or La Ceiba and connect with a daily flight to their destination, though an overnight stay may be necessary. Barbareta and the Cayos Cochinos are reachable only by boat, either from the mainland or one of the resorts offering trips to those islands.

## When Your Luggage Is Late

The Bay Islands have a reputation for poor baggage service. Though things have improved in recent years, problems still occur, particularly between connecting flights and during the holidays, when locals transport presents and supplies. A few simple tips will save you any headaches:

First, pack any essential items in your carry-on, including prescription medicines, a change of clothes, bathing suit, prescription dive mask, etc. Limit the size of the carry-on, however, as oversized bags are taken at the gate and sent later. It's best to book one of the direct flights from Miami, New Orleans or Houston. If you are connecting to a TACA flight, claim your check-in bags from the first carrier and recheck them yourself at the TACA counter—that way if the bags don't arrive, you'll at least know where to start looking.

# Getting Around

On Roatán local transportation is easy and inexpensive. Taxis and buses are based in West End, Coxen Hole, French Harbour and Oak Ridge and have defined service areas. One-way fares are US$2 per person. If you want to go outside the service area or are traveling after 6pm, the rates increase. It's best to negotiate before you hop aboard.

Taxi fares from the airport and cruise ship docks will be higher, as these are considered charter trips. The driver may charge extra if you have lots of luggage or are traveling to the far ends of the island. Cruise ship passengers must clarify whether they want a tour or service to a specific location. Again, check the rates first.

Historically, all homes and businesses were built along the shore, and transportation was by boat. Centuries ago locals hacked a waterway through the mangroves. It connects five harbors and remains a primary thoroughfare. Water taxis ferry visitors between these harbors and also connect West End and West Bay. Rates are very flexible.

Guanaja is a unique case, as there are no paved roads. Transportation is by boat, period. Water traffic is at its thickest around the bustling settlement of Bonacca, near the airport. A channel through the mangroves at the center of the island connects one side to the other.

On Utila there's only one paved road, which connects the airport to town. The main modes of transportation are by foot, bicycle, moped, golf cart or taxi.

Interisland ferry and airline services are available, with connections through La Ceiba on the mainland.

# Entry

Everyone entering Honduras must have a passport that's valid a minimum of six months beyond your date of entry into Honduras. Tourists from Australia, New Zealand, Canada, the U.S., the U.K. and most Western European countries can stay up to 30 days without a visa. Visa extensions are available for up to six months. Check with the closest Honduras consulate for specific requirements.

Upon arrival you'll pay a US$2 entry fee, and immigration officials will stamp your passport and insert a yellow visa form. To avoid a fine, hang on to this form—you must turn it in when you leave. The current departure tax is US$25, or the equivalent amount in lempira.

# Time

The Bay Islands are on Central Standard Time. Daylight saving time is not observed; during standard time, when it's noon in the Bay Islands, it's 10am in San Francisco, 1pm in New York, 6pm in London and 5am the following day in Sydney.

# Money

The official currency is the lempira (named in honor of a famous Lenca Indian chief who fought the Spanish and was treacherously murdered at the negotiation table). However, islanders gladly accept U.S. dollars and traveler's checks.

Most resorts, dive operations, restaurants and gift shops also accept credit cards, though for an additional service fee. There are no ATMs, but tourists can get cash advances on their credit cards at several banks.

# Electricity

Fairly reliable and available on most islands, electricity is 110 volts, 60 Hz AC. Roatán has its own power company, with 24-hour service. Utila draws its electricity from a single generator, which operates daily from 5am till midnight, then it's lights out. Many resorts have their own generators. Individual generators also supply power on Guanaja, Barbareta and the Cayos Cochinos.

Utilities are extremely expensive, and everyone is encouraged to limit usage. If you have a medical condition that requires an electrical device, bring a battery pack in case the power does fail. Underwater photographers should have no problem charging their equipment at major resorts and on live-aboards.

# Weights & Measures

The Bay Islands follow the imperial system of weights and measures. In this book both imperial and metric measurements are given, except for specific references in dive site descriptions, which are given in imperial units only. Please refer to the conversion chart provided on the inside back cover.

# What to Bring

## General

The islands are very casual. Pack mostly T-shirts, shorts and bathing suits. You may want to bring pants for horseback riding, boots for hiking, a sundress or nice pair of slacks for dining out and a pair of jeans and lightweight windbreaker or sweatshirt for cool summer nights. Include a raincoat if you plan to visit between October and February. Islanders tend to dress conservatively. Don't wear bathing suit tops or short shorts in town. Public nudity is forbidden.

You won't find dainty soaps, shampoos and conditioners or hair driers in your room, so bring all toiletries, including any over-the-counter or prescription medicines. Consider packing a small first-aid kit, with bandages, antibiotic cream, ear drops, motion sickness pills and decongestants. Also bring plenty of sunscreen and insect repellent. Some people are allergic to no-see-ums (biting midges), so include a strong antihistamine and hydrocortisone cream to be safe.

## Dive-Related

From April through October most divers are comfortable in a 2mm wetsuit. Many just wear a dive skin or T-shirt. After October when the water temperature drops slightly and the air is cooler, divers prefer a 2 or 3mm full wetsuit. Most resorts prohibit the use of gloves and cyalume sticks, especially in the marine reserve areas. Do bring a beach towel, dive light, camera and all the batteries and film you may need.

# Underwater Photography

Roatán offers a number of processing centers for print film, but E6 color slide processing is available only at Anthony's Key Resort. Laguna Beach Resort on Utila and the Posada del Sol on Guanaja are also set up for E6. At several resorts it's possible to hire professional videographers to record your vacation memories. Several resorts rent cameras and offer photography courses, but underwater camera rentals are limited.

# Business Hours

Banks are open weekdays from 8am to 3:30pm and till noon on Saturday. Some close for lunch. Be patient, as lines are often long and move slowly. Stores generally open by 9am and close between 5 and 6pm, again by noon on Saturday. Government offices are open weekdays from 8am to 4pm and are closed Saturday and Sunday. Restaurants often close one day a week, so check before taking off for dinner. Most businesses close on Sundays and major holidays, including Easter, Mother's Day, September 15 (Quince, or Independence Day) Christmas and New Year's Day.

Dive operators, restaurants, resorts and bars maintain hours to suit tourist requirements, although there are mandatory closing times for bars and discos. Late nights and loud music are allowed only on weekends.

# Accommodations

Bay Islands accommodations range from large dedicated dive resorts to a hammock on the beach. Visitors to Roatán select from three typical arrangements: dive resorts, rooming houses or rentals. Resorts are clustered along the east end near French Harbour, Sandy Bay and West Bay, and most offer weekly packages. Backpackers opt for less expensive digs in West End, where dive operators provide inexpensive rooms to their customers. Due to a growing need for multilingual instruction, some dive shops will even hire foreign travelers willing to trade work for housing. Other visitors rent a room, house or timeshare and then contract with either a resort or individual operator for diving services.

Guanaja is more of a Robinson Crusoe hideaway, with no roads, only two upscale resorts and several smaller operations. All specialize in diving and kayaking, and a couple offer horseback riding.

Known worldwide as one of the least expensive destinations in the Caribbean, Utila is frequented by both American and European backpackers. Rooms are available for only a few lempira. There are also several upscale dive resorts, as well as private rental homes on the offshore cays.

Barbareta and Cochino Grande are both privately owned islands with only one resort each—the Barbareta Beach Resort and Plantation Beach Resort, respectively.

# Dining & Food

Most resorts offer meal plans, though after a day of diving, visitors love to explore the local places, selecting from romantic waterfront restaurants, casual bars and bistros. Food is not the typical spicy Caribbean fare, however. Ask for a *plato típico* and you'll get simply prepared beans, rice and chicken or fish.

There are several first-class restaurants on each island, offering a variety of seafood, steaks, chicken and pasta dishes and limited but acceptable wine lists. For the budget diner, burgers, pasta and pizza are readily available. Roatán has the one and only fast-food joint. Several small restaurants feature Chinese, Thai, Italian and other international cuisine.

The Bay Islands abound with almonds, cashews, bananas, plantains, coconuts, oranges, grapefruit, mangoes, papayas, guava, berries, avocados, plums, monkey cap and more. Grocery stores and roadside stalls supply fruits, vegetables, meats, canned goods and sodas. Beer and liquor are only available in larger stores.

There is a 12% sales tax on food and a 15% sales tax on beer, liquor, cigarettes and cigars. Tips are expected, and some restaurants will add a service charge to the bill, especially for larger groups.

### What's *Not* for Dinner?

While Bay Islanders still hunt deer and iguanas, fortunately such choices are not available in local restaurants. Close to extinction, the islands' iguanas are now protected, though it's not unusual to spot an islander carrying a string of iguanas over his back. Conchs, crabs and lobsters are also protected, particularly within the marine reserves. Much of the commercial seafood is instead harvested along the offshore banks.

# Shopping

The Bay Islands are not a shopper's paradise, though you'll find any number of small businesses selling handicrafts and locally made food products. On Roatán, West End and Coxen Hole offer the better souvenir shops. Don't miss Gunter's Driftwood Gallery on Utila.

Traditional arts and crafts include intricate woodcarvings, such as masks, animals, boxes, doors and tables. Other treasures include clay bowls, hammocks and handmade crochet and embroidery. Silver and jade jewelry is abundant. Avoid buying crafts made from black coral, which is largely illegal to buy or sell. And before you buy seashells or crafts made from shells, consider that most of these animals are killed for their shells.

# Activities & Attractions

STEVE ROSENBERG

In addition to spectacular diving, the Bay Islands offer plenty of attractions, from a range of watersports to nature trails, exotic wildlife and town visits.

Most of Roatán's attractions are on the west end, though the east end offers leisurely drives through small ethnic towns such as Port Royal, Polly Tilly Bight and Punta Gorda. Guanaja's draws are centered on the resorts. The small size of Utila consolidates all activity aside from sportfishing to colorful downtown Utila, or El Centro, whose narrow streets are lined with small stores, taverns, homey restaurants and cafés, rocking nightspots and backpacker lodges. The Cayos Cochinos simply offer gorgeous views.

## Roatán Butterfly Garden

Just outside West End village, the Roatán Butterfly Garden (☎ 445-1096) is one of the island's newest attractions. The number of butterflies present depends on the season, but the enclosed garden averages 15 to 20 species, with as many as 200 individuals on any given day. The garden is open 9am to 5pm daily, except Saturdays. Admission is US$5.

## Sportfishing

You can choose from bonefishing on the reef flats or game fishing off the reef. **Laguna Beach Resort** (toll-free ☎ 800-668-8452) on Utila and the **Bay Islands Beach Resort** (☎ 445-1425) and **Bonefish Lodge** (www.bonefishlodge.com) on Roatán are the favorites among hardcore anglers. The larger resorts all offer half- and full-day trips to try your luck landing jacks, wahoos, king mackerel, barracuda and tuna. On Guanaja check out **Capt. J.C. Morgan** and his boat, the *Hillbilly* (toll-free ☎ 800-535-7063).

## Tropical Treasures Bird Park

Tropical Treasures Bird Park (☎ 445-1314) was originally a small private collection. This outdoor aviary now houses one of the most complete parrot collections in Central America, as well as colorful macaws and toucans. You can wander at your own pace in the shade of tall mango trees or join an informative guided tour. Based in Roatán's Sandy Bay, the park is open Tuesday to Sunday 10am to 5pm.

# Carambola Botanical Gardens

Also in Sandy Bay on Roatán, Carambola Botanical Gardens & Nature Trails (☎ 445-1117) shelters hundreds of tropical plants, most of which are identified for the lay botanist. You'll find banana and chocolate trees, jungle cactus and hibiscus, as well as native medicinal plants growing in wild clusters. Garden aficionados are particularly awed by the impressive collection of heliconias and palms. There are two trails to choose from—the Mountain Path and the Jungle Path—each of which takes about 15 minutes. The gardens are open daily from 7am to 5pm. Admission is US$3.

MICHAEL LAWRENCE

# Wild Cane Historic Village

This open-air museum at the Bay Islands Beach Resort in Sandy Bay depicts what life was like on Roatán more than a century ago. You'll tour traditional handmade cane and mud houses, a medicine garden and a farm, as islanders share stories and folklore about island life, medicines, food and family. Also on display is a traditional wooden dugout fishing boat, or *cayuco*. At the weekly village party, visitors can sample regional food made in handmade mud stoves. The village is open daily 9am to 4pm. You can take a self-guided walk or contact the resort (☎ 445-1425) to arrange a tour. Tours are US$5, while a Tuesday night tour and dinner costs US$10.

# Mangrove Tour

Before there were roads on Roatán, Indians used dugout canoes to travel between villages on the east end. As high seas made ocean passages uncomfortable, they carved out a waterway through the mangroves, connecting five harbors. It remains well traveled. Locals scurry about their business in outboards and dugouts and on Jet Skis. You can hire a water taxi out of Jonesville, Oak Ridge or Calabash Bight and explore the homes, shops, fishing boats, swimming holes and private lake along this waterway. Special trips are also available from Oak Ridge to Port Royal.

## Trees With Legs

Mangroves are complex shoreline habitats formed by the massive root systems of several species of salt-tolerant trees and shrubs, including species of *Rhizophora*, *Avicennia* and *Laguncularia*. These are largely self-sufficient ecosystems that control soil erosion and provide shelter to a wide range of marine life and birds. While inshore waters are often murky, the outer mangroves offer good snorkeling and are brimming with juvenile fish, sponges, corals and other invertebrates.

DAVID BEHRENS

# Dolphin Encounter

The Roatán Institute for Marine Sciences (☎ 445-1327), at Anthony's Key Resort in Sandy Bay, offers wonderful opportunities to learn about and interact with dolphins. Under the supervision of trained handlers, waders, swimmers, snorkelers and divers of all ages can swim alongside dolphins, stroke them, play with them and marvel at this marine mammal's intelligence. A videographer is available to record your encounter. Several programs are available and are offered three times a day between 8:30am and 3:30pm. Reservations are mandatory and should be made three to four days in advance.

STEVE ROSENBERG

Playful bottlenose dolphins are free to roam among curious snorkelers.

# Horseback Riding

You'll find riding stables on the larger islands. On Roatán, Keifito's Plantation resort offers a two-hour horse trek that takes you into the hills and along the beach at West Bay. Most trips are suitable for riders of all experience levels. Make arrangements through your resort.

# Iguana Farm

Once among the most abundant land animals in the Bay Islands, iguanas have been hunted to near extinction from the region. Although it is prohibited by Honduran law, islanders still kill the reptile for food. One family is striving to reverse the population demise.

Pay a visit to the iguana farm, in French Cay on Roatán, where Sherman Arch and his family raise these magnificent reptiles. The grounds are crawling with hundreds of iguanas of all ages and several species. Visit at noon to assist in feeding the lot. There is a suggested US$1 donation to assist the family with their noble cause. The farm is open daily 9am to 5pm.

# Natural Aquarium Snorkel Trail

This underwater trail at the Bay Islands Beach Resort (☎ 445-1425), in Sandy Bay on Roatán, allows snorkelers of every age and skill level to view distinct reef habitats and the creatures that live there. Marked by buoys, 12 stations guide you across lush coral heads, turtle grass beds and sand flats, where you'll encounter everything from gorgonians, sea stars and squid to eagle rays, trumpetfish, goatfish, schools of damsels and sergeant majors and more. Night on the trail brings out lobsters, octopuses and shrimp of every variety. The trail is open daily 9am to 4:30pm. Guided night tours run between 6 and 10pm. Admission is US$15.

Bonacca's docks are the center of village life.

# Bonacca

Nearly the entire population of Guanaja lives in the overwater community of Bonacca, built atop a submerged cay just east of the airport. Narrow walkways and bridges connect the hundreds of colorful shanties that comprise the carefree village. Wander the docks to meet the friendly townsfolk and admire their traditional wooden dugout canoes.

# Diving Health & Safety

STEVE ROSENBERG

The Bay Islands are a safe destination and pose few health risks to most visitors. As is the case throughout the Caribbean, the biggest danger is the tropical sun. Use waterproof sunblock and wear protective clothing to avoid sunburn, and drink plenty of water to prevent dehydration. Tap water is safe to drink at the larger resorts, otherwise bottled water is available at all small restaurants and stores. If you plan a long stay or trips to more remote areas, consult your physician about suggested vaccinations and be sure to pack any needed prescription drugs.

More of a problem during the rainy season, mosquitoes, sand flies and voracious no-see-ums (biting midges) cause some visitors aggravation. You should come armed with plenty of insect repellent. Anyone allergic to insect bites should ask his or her doctor for prednisone tablets, just in case. Cases of two mosquito-borne diseases, malaria and dengue fever, have been reported in the Bay Islands. Consider taking a course of antimalarial tablets, though divers may experience adverse reactions. There is no prophylactic available to combat dengue; simply do your best to avoid being bitten.

The U.S. Centers for Disease Control & Prevention regularly posts updates on health-related concerns around the world specifically for travelers. Contact the CDC by fax or visit their website. Call (toll-free from the U.S.) ☎ 888-232-3299 and request Document 000005 to receive a list of documents available by fax. The web site is www.cdc.gov.

## Diving & Flying

Most divers in the Bay Islands arrive by plane. While it's fine to dive soon *after* flying, it's important to remember that your last dive should be completed at least 24 hours *before* your flight to minimize the risk of decompression sickness, caused by residual nitrogen in the blood.

# Pre-Trip Preparation

Your general state of health, diving skill level and specific equipment needs are the three most important factors that impact any dive trip. If you honestly assess these before you leave, you'll be well on your way to assuring a safe dive trip.

MICHAEL MCKAY

Use a marker tube to signal the boat if you are separated from it.

First, if you're not in shape, start exercising. Second, if you haven't dived for a while (six months is too long), and your skills are rusty, do a local dive with an experienced buddy or take a scuba review course. Feeling good physically and diving regularly will make you a safer diver and enhance your enjoyment underwater.

At least a month before your trip, inspect your dive gear. Remember, your regulator should be serviced annually, whether you've used it or not. If you use a dive computer and can replace the battery yourself, change it before the trip or buy a spare one to take along. Otherwise, send the computer to the manufacturer for a battery replacement.

If possible, find out if the dive center you'll be using rents or services the type of gear you own. If not, you might want to take spare parts or even spare gear. A spare mask is always a good idea.

Purchase any additional equipment you might need, such as a dive light and tank marker light for night diving, a line reel for wreck diving, etc. Make sure you have at least a whistle attached to your BC. Better yet, add a marker tube (also known as a safety sausage or come-to-me) and an air horn.

About a week before taking off, do a final check of your gear, grease o-rings, check batteries and assemble a save-a-dive kit. This kit should at minimum contain spare mask and fin straps, snorkel keeper, mouthpiece, valve cap, zip ties and o-rings.

# Tips for Evaluating a Dive Operator

First impressions mean a lot. Does the business appear organized and professionally staffed? Does it prominently display a dive affiliation such as NAUI, PADI, SSI etc.? These are both good indications that it adheres to high standards.

When you come to dive, a well-run business will always have paperwork for you to fill out. At the least, someone should look at your certification card and ask when you last dived. If they want to see your logbook or check basic skills in the water, even better.

Rental equipment should be well rinsed. If you see sand or salt crystals, watch out, as their presence could indicate sloppy equipment care. Before starting on your dive, inspect the equipment thoroughly: Check hoses for wear, see that mouthpieces are secure and make sure they've given you a depth gauge and air pressure gauge.

After you gear up and turn on your air, listen for air leaks. Now test your BC: Push the power inflator to make sure it functions correctly and doesn't free-flow; if it fails, get another BC—don't try to inflate it manually; make sure the BC holds air. Then purge your regulator a bit and smell the air. It should be odorless. If you detect an oily or otherwise bad smell, try a different tank, then start searching for another operator.

# DAN

Divers Alert Network (DAN) is an international membership association of individuals and organizations sharing a common interest in diving and safety. It operates a 24-hour diving emergency hot line in the U.S.: ☎ **919-684-8111 or 919-684-4DAN** (-4326). The latter accepts collect calls in a dive emergency. Though DAN does not directly provide medical care, it does provide advice on early treatment, evacuation and hyperbaric treatment of diving-related injuries. Divers should contact DAN for assistance as soon as a diving emergency is suspected.

DAN membership is reasonably priced and includes DAN TravelAssist, a membership benefit that covers medical air evacuation from anywhere in the world for any illness or injury. For a small additional fee, divers can get secondary insurance coverage for decompression illness. For membership details contact DAN at ☎ 800 446-2671 in the U.S. or ☎ 919-684-2948 elsewhere. DAN can also be reached at www.diversalertnetwork.org.

# Medical & Recompression Facilities

The Bay Islands' main medical facilities are in Coxen Hole on Roatán (where there are two hospitals) and on the mainland in La Ceiba, with smaller medical clinics on Guanaja and Utila. Although you will find pharmacies, it's a good idea to bring sufficient medication for your needs, as foreign prescriptions will not be filled.

Hyperbaric chambers are available on Roatán at both Anthony's Key Resort and Fantasy Island, and on Utila at the Utila Lodge, which was rebuilt following a fire in 2001. There are no chambers on Guanaja or the smaller islands.

## Medical Contacts

### Hospitals
Roatán
Roatán Hospital (public)
☎ 445-1499
Woods Hospital (private)
☎ 445-1850

### Medical Clinics
Guanaja
☎ 453-4472
Utila
☎ 425-3277

### Hyperbaric Chambers
Roatán
Anthony's Key Resort
☎ 445-1049
Fantasy Island
☎ 455-5222

Utila
Utila Lodge
☎ 425-3143

DAVID BEHRENS

# Diving in Honduras' Bay Islands

MICHAEL LAWRENCE

The Bay Islands are famous for world-class wall diving, though the islands' leeward sides offer plenty of shallow sites that will please both snorkelers and divers. You'll also find several ships sunk deliberately as artificial reefs, such as the *Prince Albert* and the *Águila* off Roatán, the *Halliburton* off Utila and the *Jado Trader* off Guanaja. Scattered throughout the islands are several smaller wrecks, including two airplanes.

The fringing reefs off Roatán, Barbareta, Guanaja and Utila lie approximately 300ft (90m) offshore and are easily accessed from land. For convenience, however, most of the islands' dive operators visit the reefs by boat. The proximity of the reefs means a mere five to 10-minute boat ride to most sites. Boats tie to appropriate moorings either inside or outside the reef. Some popular drift-diving sites lack moorings, in which case your boat will drift with you and pick you up where you surface.

There are several dive centers and a dozen or so resorts on Roatán, while Barbareta has only one resort, and Guanaja and Utila have only a handful. The Cayos Cochinos are accessed by daytrip dive boats from the mainland and Utila.

There is currently only one live-aboard in the Bay Islands, the *Bay Islands Aggressor IV*, which is based at the Parrot Tree Plantation Resort at Second Bight, on the central coast of Roatán. A typical seven-day trip circles Roatán and visits Barbareta, Guanaja and Cayos Cochinos.

Bay Islands reefs share similar characteristics. Between the beach and the open ocean are a number of topographic features, each providing habitat for different species. Farthest from shore is the reef wall, which plunges steeply to great depths. Here the plankton- and nutrient-rich water sustains the lush reefs and carries a continuous influx of marine species' eggs and larvae from throughout the Caribbean, adding to the region's biological diversity.

In general, the steep drop-offs begin in about 50ft (15m) of water. This area is referred to as the buttress or reef front. This portion of the outer reef slopes gently shoreward to the reef crest, which is often marked by breaking waves. Usually, the crest is about a foot (60cm) underwater and passable only in a few places.

Behind the reef crest is the reef flat or lagoon. In the Bay Islands this area rarely exceeds 15ft (5m) in depth and features scattered coral heads surrounded by sand and seagrass. Seagrass beds dominate the shallows.

The following regional sections provide brief descriptions of the most popular and accessible sites throughout the islands. To make the most out of the diving opportunities in each region, group your dives along a single shoreline, allowing time for an adequate surface interval and the opportunity to visit two or three different sites each day.

# Dive Training & Certification

The Bay Islands are certainly among the best places in the world to learn to scuba dive. Taking your Open Water class in the warm clear Caribbean is like learning in a pool. Most Bay Islands dive resorts and operators employ qualified NAUI and PADI instructors and offer a variety of classes, from Open Water to refresher, advanced and specialty courses.

## EANx: The Nitrox Solution

Enriched air nitrox (EANx) is available only on Roatán. Although it's a little more expensive than a regular tank fill, it's easy to get on the island.

The mixture used in the Bay Islands is almost exclusively EANx32, which means it's 32% oxygen. The Bay Islands Beach Resort offers both 32 and 36% mixtures. Since normal tank fills are 21% oxygen, you'll be getting more oxygen and less nitrogen into your system. Nitrox can increase bottom times, but most divers in Bay Islands use it for the extra safety margin and because they say it makes them feel better. Certainly, with less nitrogen and more oxygen in your system, you'll decrease your risk of decompression sickness, though there is increased risk of oxygen toxicity at depth.

If you're nitrox certified, be sure to bring your certification card. If you're not certified, you can take one of the many nitrox classes offered by dive operators on Roatán.

Utila is reputed to be the cheapest place on the planet to get certified—sometimes less than US$100 per person. The cost of taking an Open Water course varies greatly, however, depending on the number of enrolled students.

Beyond the basics, courses in entry-level nitrox (a two-day course with two dives) and advanced nitrox (a two-day course with four dives) are available. A course in decompression techniques (four days, six dives) is taught at some resorts. Pre-dive qualification is required for all advanced courses.

# Snorkeling

Although scuba diving is the region's main attraction, there are also many wonderful snorkeling opportunities for nondivers as well as divers who have reached their daily nitrogen limit but want to see more.

House reefs off many of the resorts promise great daytime and nighttime snorkeling adventures. Some resorts offer dedicated snorkeling classes and excursions.

On Roatán the reef flats along both sides of the island boast all the habitat and species diversity of the outer reef. Utila and Guanaja have similar shallow-water spots within their fringing reefs. You'll also find good snorkeling off Barbareta and Cayos Cochinos and their various cays.

Shallow reef flats offer easy and rewarding snorkeling.

## Dive Site Icons

The symbols at the beginning of each dive site description provide a quick summary of some of the following characteristics present at each site:

 Good snorkeling or free-diving site.

 Remains or partial remains of a wreck can be seen at this site.

 Sheer wall or drop-off.

 Deep dive. Features of this dive occur in water deeper than 27m (90ft).

 Strong currents may be encountered at this site.

 Strong surge (the horizontal movement of water caused by waves) may be encountered at this site.

 Drift dive. Because of strong currents and/or difficulty in anchoring, a drift dive is recommended at this site.

Beach/shore dive. This site can be accessed from shore.

 Poor visibility. The site often has visibility of less than 12m (40ft).

 Caves are a prominent feature of this site. Only experienced cave divers should explore inner cave areas.

 Marine preserve. Special regulations apply in this area.

# Pisces Rating System for Dives & Divers

The dive sites in this book are rated according to the following diver skill-level rating system. These are not absolute ratings but apply to divers at a particular time, diving at a particular place. For instance, someone unfamiliar with prevailing conditions might be considered a novice diver at one dive area, but an intermediate diver at another, more familiar location.

**Novice:** A novice diver should be accompanied by an instructor, divemaster or advanced diver on all dives. A novice diver generally fits the following profile:
◆ basic scuba certification from an internationally recognized certifying agency
◆ dives infrequently (less than one trip a year)
◆ logged fewer than 25 total dives
◆ little or no experience diving in similar waters and conditions
◆ dives no deeper than 60ft (18m)

**Intermediate:** An intermediate diver generally fits the following profile:
◆ may have participated in some form of continuing diver education
◆ logged between 25 and 100 dives
◆ dives no deeper than 130ft (40m)
◆ has been diving in similar waters and conditions within the last six months

**Advanced:** An advanced diver generally fits the following profile:
◆ advanced certification
◆ has been diving for more than two years and logged over 100 dives
◆ has been diving in similar waters and conditions within the last six months

Regardless of your skill level, you should be in good physical condition and know your limitations. If you are uncertain of your own level of expertise for a particular site, ask the advice of a local dive instructor. He or she is best qualified to assess your abilities based on the site's prevailing dive conditions. Ultimately, however, you must decide if you are capable of making a particular dive, a decision that should take into account your level of training, recent experience and physical condition, as well as the conditions at the site. Remember that conditions can change at any time, even during a dive.

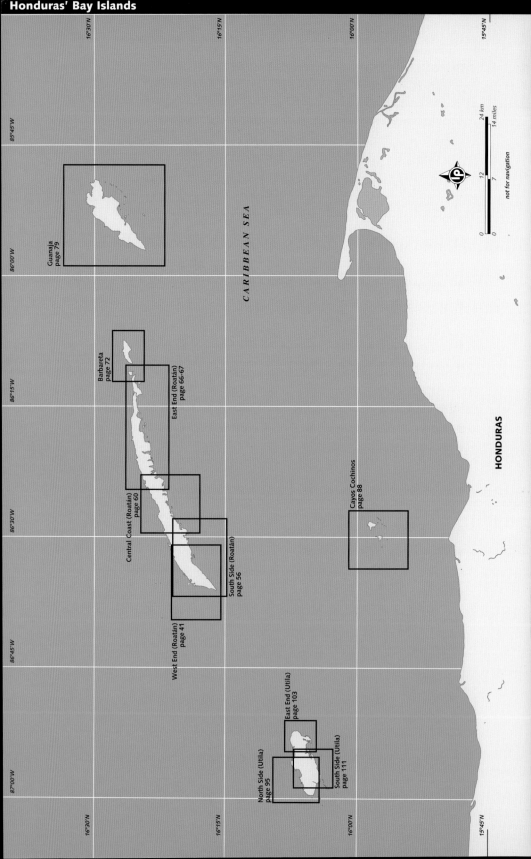

# Roatán Dive Sites

The largest of the Bay Islands, Roatán is also considered the tourism hub, thanks to its well-developed dive industry. Its dozen or so dive resorts and operations all offer full packages, including a range of accommodations, the latest in rental equipment, and boat dives throughout local waters. While resorts schedule most dives nearby, each offers longer daytrips.

The island's 90-plus moorings mark only about a third of the possible dive sites. About half of the sites are clustered along the island's west end. The northwestern shore is lined with a series of resorts and diver-friendly rentals, from Sandy Bay to the bohemian village of West End, where limits on commercial harvesting have helped to preserve the island's robust marine life. There are also a number of dive sites along the central coast between French Harbour and Oak Ridge, as well as a few remote east end sites.

You'll find spectacular wall and drift dives on both the north and south shores, and reef flats along either shore allow snorkelers and swimmers easy access to the outer reef wall. Water temperatures range from the high 70s Fahrenheit (about 25°C) in winter to the mid-80s Fahrenheit (about 30°C) in summer. Visibility at most locations is at least 75ft (23m), though under the right conditions it can reach 150ft (46m).

Visitors are lured to Roatán by its lush slopes, powdery beaches and miles of reefs.

## West End

West End village is the center of action on the island. Dive operators, discos, bars, gift shops, hotels, rooming houses and small beaches line the 2-mile (3km) stretch of unpaved road that parallels the shoreline. Divers can simply browse the dive shops and select one that meets their needs. Don't miss the Roatán Butterfly Garden, just outside of town.

South of the village, West Bay boasts a beautiful horseshoe-shaped white-sand beach with nearshore reefs. Once pristine and undeveloped, the area is now home to condos, time-shares, resorts and visiting cruise ship passengers.

Between Gibson Bight and Sandy Bay are several excellent dive resorts and quiet restaurants. Sandy Bay has one of the longest natural beaches on the island. Other attractions include the dolphin encounter at Anthony's Key Resort, the snorkeling trail at Bay Islands Beach Resort and the Tropical Treasures Bird Park.

All dive sites along the west end are within the Sandy Bay–West End Marine Reserve. No commercial fishing, lobstering or conch collecting is allowed in the reserve. Sites stretch from Sandy Bay to West End Point. Most of the 40-odd moored dive sites along this shoreline are wall dives. If you only have time to dive a few sites, try West End Wall, Hole in the Wall, the wreck of the *Águila* and Barry's Reef.

## West End Dive Sites

| | Good Snorkeling | Novice | Intermediate | Advanced |
|---|---|---|---|---|
| 1 Herbie's Place | | | ● | |
| 2 West End Wall | | | ● | |
| 3 Herbie's Fantasy | ● | ● | | |
| 4 Sea Quest | ● | ● | | |
| 5 Blue Channel | ● | ● | | |
| 6 Lighthouse Reef | | ● | | |
| 7 Half Moon Bay Wall | | ● | | |
| 8 Divemaster's Choice | ● | ● | | |
| 9 Hole in the Wall | | | ● | |
| 10 Canyon Reef | | ● | | |
| 11 Fish Den | | ● | | |
| 12 Gibson Bight | | ● | | |
| 13 Overheat Reef | | ● | | |
| 14 Águila | | | ● | |
| 15 Peter's Place | | ● | | |
| 16 Bear's Den | | | ● | |
| 17 Spooky Channel | ● | | ● | |
| 18 Barry's Reef | ● | ● | | |

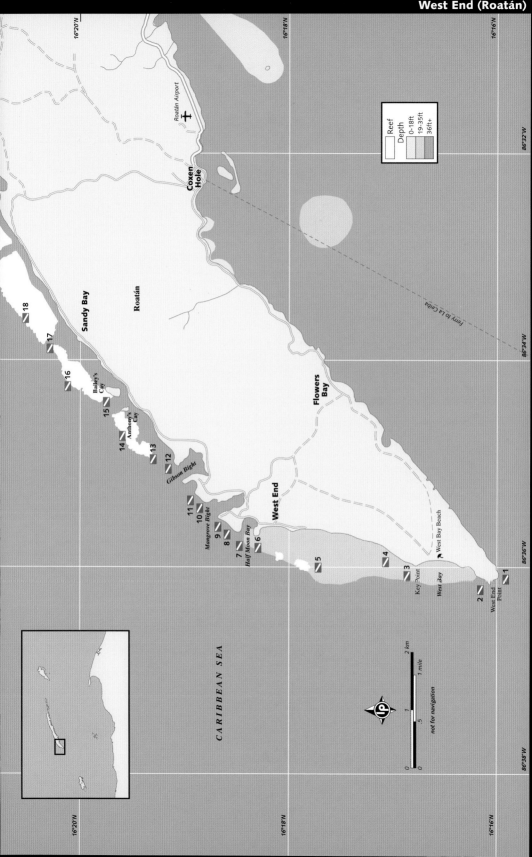

## 1 Herbie's Place

Like West End Wall to the north, Herbie's Place is an awesome drift dive. The direction you drift depends on prevailing currents and tides. If you drift east from the point along the south side, you'll end up near **Pablo's Place**, another great dive spot.

This site's spectacular panorama is broken by deep cuts in the wall and by

**Location:** Southern tip of West End Point

**Depth Range:** 20-130ft+ (6-40m+)

**Access:** Boat

**Expertise Rating:** Intermediate

several large sand patches. Among other marine life, you'll find huge barrel sponges. To find one of the resident seahorses, search the bases of sea fans and other gorgonians along the crest of the wall.

One curious species that always seems to pop up is the tiny arrow blenny. Little more than an inch long, this species doesn't sit on the substrate like other blenny species; instead, it hovers in the water column, its tail bent back toward its head. This odd posture allows the fish to dart away when alarmed or when capturing small prey.

If you want to photograph turtles, you're in the right place. You may also spot large pelagics such as barracuda, tarpon, crevalle jacks and groupers.

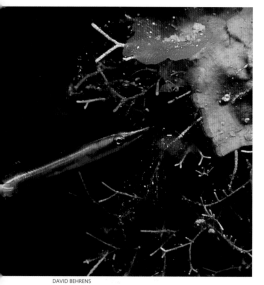

DAVID BEHRENS

An arrow blenny cocks its tail, ready to strike.

## 2 West End Wall

This is one of the premier dives on Roatán. You'll likely drift dive this site, as the current is usually running in one direction or another. When the currents are right and the lighting good, this site offers great wide-angle photo opportunities.

You have a choice to either drift over the reef edge, enjoying the magnitude of the wall, or move in close to look for seahorses that hide at the base of sea rods, sea whips and sea fans. Look carefully, as

**Location:** Just north of West End Point

**Depth Range:** 10-130ft+ (3-40m+)

**Access:** Boat

**Expertise Rating:** Intermediate

the longsnout seahorse is a master of disguise and blends in amid the gorgonians.

The large barrel sponges and pillar corals on this portion of the reef are quite spectacular. The Bay Islands are home to several species of barrel sponge—the giant barrel, leathery barrel and netted barrel.

You're almost guaranteed a turtle or two on this dive, and keep your eyes open for spotted eagle rays and schools of tarpon, jacks and barracuda. If you're diving the site in spring, give a wide berth to the large ocean triggerfish guarding their nests. If you come too close, expect to be chased off by a defensive parent with prominent front teeth.

MICHAEL LAWRENCE

Giant barrel sponges grow a mere half inch per year.

## 3  Herbie's Fantasy

Named after a divemaster from Anthony's Key Resort, Herbie's Fantasy is an excellent shallow-water site for snorkelers and novice divers. Largely a sandy area, the site boasts beautiful coral heads and ridges in about 40ft of water. Camouflaged in the sand are various bottom-dwelling species, including flounder, stingrays and huge horse conchs. Resident coral species include pencil coral (*Madracis*), boulder star coral (*Montastraea*) and fire coral. On the coral outcrops you'll find sea fans, whip corals and numerous sponge species.

**Location:** Inner reef off Key Point

**Depth Range:** 10-40ft (3-12m)

**Access:** Boat or shore

**Expertise Rating:** Novice

One common sponge, the branching tube sponge (*Pseudoceratina*), comes in a variety of shapes and colors, giving the appearance of being several species. You can usually tell this sponge by its yellow exterior with purple or green overcoat.

The site also attracts triggerfish, parrotfish, barracuda and a few small groupers. Trumpetfish, a solitary species, are common among the soft corals, as are flamingo tongue snails, which graze on sea fans.

Branching tube sponges sport spectacular shapes and colors.

## 4 Sea Quest

Just northeast of Herbie's Fantasy, Sea Quest is another shallow dive site that's perfect for snorkelers and novice divers. It's also an excellent night dive. Wide-angle photographers will appreciate the shallow depth and good light penetration.

There are a variety of reef and sand habitats to investigate. As you swim above the shallow coral heads, you'll see numerous species of damselfish and wrasses seeking refuge in the reef crannies.

The dominant coral species at Sea Quest is fire coral, which grows in two distinct morphological forms: a branched

**Location:** Inner reef north of Key Point

**Depth Range:** 10-40ft (3-12m)

**Access:** Boat or shore

**Expertise Rating:** Novice

treelike form and a flat, paddle-shaped form. While both produce beautiful outcrops full of fish and other reef species, they will give you a painful sting if you rub against them. To see what makes this coral sting, look carefully at the tan-colored surface. You'll see tiny pores and fine, hairlike projections nearly invisible to the unaided eye.

The burning sensation from a sting only lasts for several minutes, but may produce red welts on the skin. Do not rub the affected area, as you'll only spread the stinging particles. Cortisone cream will reduce the inflammation, and antihistamine cream is good for killing the pain. To avoid being stung, regard this coral's beauty from a distance.

A fire coral's fine "hairs" are actually stinging cells.

## 5  Blue Channel

Blue Channel is a shallow dive spot with a shore entry opposite Sueño del Mar Dive Center. The channel runs parallel to shore and is about 30ft deep. There are a number of small caves along its south wall. Beware of fire coral in the shallows.

Reef life here is diverse. Thick schools of damselfish and tangs circle the waters above the reef, calling to mind Grand Central Station at rush hour. Grunts, snappers and young groupers frequent the reef and channel, and small fish of every color dart to and fro. Juvenile barracuda patrol the reef, perhaps in training for the move to deeper water.

Shallow-water sites like Blue Channel host many examples of reef species prac-

**Location:** Offshore from Sueño del Mar Dive Center

**Depth Range:** 5-50ft (2-15m)

**Access:** Boat or shore

**Expertise Rating:** Novice

ticing photosynthesis—converting the sun's energy into sugars and other nutrients. In simple terms, they've become "solar powered" to feed themselves. In corals like the cactus coral, single-celled algae called zooxanthellae take shelter in the coral's polyps, which during the day are fully extended, soaking up the sunlight and in turn nourishing the coral. Some nudibranchs remove the cell sap from algae on which they feed, keeping it alive to also benefit from the byproducts of photosynthesis.

## 6 Lighthouse Reef

Lighthouse Reef is a good basic wall dive. You descend at the mooring to a sand bottom only 15ft deep. Several large sand patches are home to peacock flounder, spotted eagle rays, stingrays, goatfish, triggerfish and bottom-dwelling invertebrates such as sea urchins and large conchs. Coral heads bordering the patches are lush with sponges and gorgonians. Look closely to spot cleaner shrimp and nudibranchs.

The reef crest is at 40ft. About 80ft seaward from the mooring the wall drops, descending to 110ft. Off the wall you'll see the familiar pelagics, including barracuda, turtles and schooling jacks.

Thanks to its shallow mooring and protected location, Lighthouse Reef is also a great night dive. The reef comes

**Location:** Off the south lip of Half Moon Bay

**Depth Range:** 15-110ft (5-34m)

**Access:** Boat

**Expertise Rating:** Novice

alive like you've never seen it before, as many coral species extend their polyps to feed only at night. Other nocturnal species include large red basket stars, which cling to sea fans. Red night shrimp and Caribbean and spotted spiny lobsters are also more active, despite the threat from foraging octopuses, also searching the reef for a meal.

## 7 Half Moon Bay Wall

Half Moon Bay is a roughly crescent-shaped bay just north of West End village. The wall is semicircular, beginning at 20ft and sloping gradually to about 60ft. At that depth you'll reach a shelf that extends to the edge of the drop-off. The wall bottoms out below 130ft. When a current is present, this is a good drift dive.

This site offers a particularly good demonstration of how species stratify by depth. The shallows host largely hard corals, sea fans and other soft corals, while deeper on the drop-off, sponges such as large barrel, elephant ear and azure vase dominate.

**Location:** Just outside Half Moon Bay

**Depth Range:** 20-130ft+ (6-40m+)

**Access:** Boat

**Expertise Rating:** Novice

Fish life includes every known local species. Especially abundant are blue tangs, smallmouth and French grunts, queen and French angelfish, spotfin and foureye butterflyfish, blue chromis and a few green morays. You may also encounter a few resident groupers, among them black and tiger groupers and large red hinds. Close examination of the coral heads reveals a completely different community of fish, that of the gobies, blennies and triplefins. Fairy basslet, juvenile drum and young trunkfish are commonplace in the holes on the face of the wall.

Resident black groupers cruise the reef.

## 8 Divemaster's Choice

Divemaster's Choice is a great snorkeling site for guests at Seagrape Plantation Resort and others having permission to cross the resort grounds. Steps lead down the black karst shoreline to the water, and it's a short swim from there to one of the most productive reefs in the Sandy Bay–West End Marine Reserve. For those diving from a boat, the mooring is atop the gently sloping wall in about 25ft of water.

**Location:** Offshore from Seagrape Plantation Resort

**Depth Range:** 10-110ft (3-34m)

**Access:** Boat or shore

**Expertise Rating:** Novice

It's best to drift dive along the crest of the wall, where you'll find larger coral species such as elkhorn, pillar, brain and starlet, as well as patches of scroll and sheet corals. You'll also spot a wide vari-

ety of sponges, from several species of ball sponges to larger encrusting sponges.

Look for the orange icing sponge, which encrusts the underside of several

corals, particularly star corals. This sponge seems to modify a coral's growth, giving its edges a scalloped appearance.

Honeycomb cowfish, white-spotted filefish and Spanish hogfish are common here. Peer beneath the ledges to find schools of bridle cardinalfish, as well as both reef and longspine squirrelfish.

Wreathing the coral heads are orange icing sponges.

## 9  Hole in the Wall

As the name implies, Hole in the Wall is a series of caves and chutes that cut through the reef and exit on the wall at various depths. The mooring at this site is in about 20ft of water.

To reach the largest cave, follow the crevicelike canyon northeast from the base of the mooring. You'll reach a wide chute that will drop you all the way to 140ft. Monitor your gauges and be aware of your depth. Advanced divers will especially enjoy exploring this cave, where you'll find schools of silversides and glassy sweepers, schoolmasters, black corals and various crystal-colored hydroids.

As at other sheer walls on this side of the island, nocturnal species are preva-

**Location:** West of Mangrove Bight

**Depth Range:** 20-130ft+ (6-40m+)

**Access:** Boat

**Expertise Rating:** Intermediate

lent. Overhangs and crevices shelter every known species of squirrelfish in the Caribbean, as well as glasseye snappers and barred cardinalfish. Other residents of the wall include spotted drum and goldentail morays. Also keep an eye out for large groupers, turtles, barracuda and spotted eagle rays.

## 10  Canyon Reef

Another good drift dive, Canyon Reef boasts unique terrain. The wall is cut with large crevices that resemble deep canyons or ravines. When currents are absent, take a moment to swim out from the reef and glance back. Divers don't often venture into blue water to enjoy the spectacular views.

Along the reef crest, gorgonians and sea fans provide perfect habitat for seahorses, trumpetfish, filefish and turtles.

**Location:** East of Mangrove Bight

**Depth Range:** 10-130ft+ (3-40m+)

**Access:** Boat

**Expertise Rating:** Novice

Atop and along the wall, look for huge barrel sponges, large rope sponges and black corals. Species such as lobsters and spotted and green morays typically lay low until nightfall, when they come out to forage more securely on the reef face.

Numerous cleaning stations pepper the wall. Here commensal and pepper-mint shrimp prompt parasite-infested customers to stop by for a cleaning. The stations are also manned by cleaner gobies, which rush from the reef to compete with the shrimp for supper, as they swim in and out of the client's mouth and gills.

Giant barrel sponges lining the wall can be 60 to 80 years old.

## 11 Fish Den

This typical north shore wall site is approachable as a drift or an out-and-back dive. As its name suggests, Fish Den is a favorite gathering place for lots of fish. Exceptional sponge and soft-coral growth probably explains the population density.

Among the species you'll find is the blue tang, a fish that changes color as it grows. Solitary swimmers, juveniles are bright yellow. As they mature, the body turns blue, except for the tail, which remains yellow. Adults are entirely blue and school in large aggregations.

**Location:** West of Gibson Bight

**Depth Range:** 10-130ft+ (3-40m+)

**Access:** Boat

**Expertise Rating:** Novice

Similar color-changing species to look for include the cocoa damselfish (juveniles are blue and yellow, while adults are dusky brown) and gray angelfish (juveniles are black with vertical yellow bars, while adults are uniform gray).

Other fish are harder to spot. Slender trumpetfish hover vertically to blend in with swaying sea rods, while spotted scorpionfish lie motionless in a mossy heap, hoping to surprise unwary swimmers-by.

Juvenile blue tangs are, oddly, a striking yellow.

## 12 Gibson Bight

Gibson Bight features a shallow wall that's suitable for divers of all experience levels. The wall is broken into numerous channels and canyons. From the mooring you swim down a small canyon to the edge of the drop-off. The diverse habitats support a variety of species.

Densely covered with soft corals and sponges, the reef is teeming with parrotfish, triggerfish, filefish, angelfish and wrasses. Spotted eagle rays feed in the bight—glance up from the wall to observe them gliding overhead.

While the sand bottom may seem devoid of life, closer inspection will surprise you. In the sand channels you may find peacock and eyed flounder and

**Location:** Offshore from namesake bight

**Depth Range:** 50-90ft (15-27m)

**Access:** Boat

**Expertise Rating:** Novice

small stingrays. Small schools of yellow goatfish and sand tilefish forage atop the sand, followed by solitary hogfish. Also look for yellowhead jawfish and soft-bottom invertebrates such as sand dollars, spaghetti worms, lugworms, mantis shrimp and queen and horse conchs.

## 13    Overheat Reef

This site has something for everyone. A great novice dive site, it also offers a spectacular drop-off and a large pinnacle for the more advanced diver. The mooring is near the wall in about 15ft of water.

In the shallows you'll find a grotto known for large clinging crabs and spiny lobsters. It also boasts a colorful collection of encrusting and vase sponges. Many of these species encrust dead coral branches and take on interesting shapes, while others grow beneath overhangs. This is where you'll find the smaller, translucent calcareous sponges. These crevices also shelter colonies of lacy pink *Stylaster* hydrocorals, whose delicate branches would be unable to survive on the open reef.

**Location:** East of Gibson Bight

**Depth Range:** 15-130ft+ (5-40m+)

**Access:** Boat

**Expertise Rating:** Novice

The pinnacle is about a five-minute swim west of the mooring along the face of the wall. Depending on the currents, this can be a nice drift dive. The reef crest here is thick with star, brain and pillar corals, and gorgonians are abundant. Keep an eye on the blue for schools of horse-eye and crevalle jacks, spadefish and pelagics such as cero and barracuda.

## 14    *Águila*

The wreck of the scuttled *Águila* (Eagle) is on the north side of the island in about 95ft of water. Some operators refer to the site as the **Eagle Wreck**. The hull lies on its starboard side about 100ft from the base of the wall.

Prior to Hurricane Mitch the wreck was a good dive, though because the hull was fairly intact, it was a challenge to see much more than the outside of the ship. The forces of Mitch, however, have made this a great dive, breaking the hull into three sections, allowing divers easy access to view resident marine life. This is one example where you can say Mitch actually improved a dive site.

The steel hull provides hundreds of square yards of

**Location:** West of Anthony's Cay

**Depth Range:** 25-95ft (8-29m)

**Access:** Boat

**Expertise Rating:** Intermediate

DAVID BEHRENS

The hull hosts cup corals, tunicates and other colonials.

real estate for encrusting organisms such as sponges, bryozoans, scallops, colorful algae and plate corals. The presence of these species has in turn attracted grazers and foragers, both fish and invertebrates. You'll find snails, nudibranchs, shrimp, sea stars and dozens of grazing damselfish and parrotfish. The piping, rigging and many corners, holes and compartments serve as a veritable marine life metropolis.

On the sand bottom between the wreck and the wall is a colony of garden eels, and peacock flounders and sting-rays are common. After investigating the wreck, swim to the reef to complete your dive in shallower water. The wall is cut with deep canyons, home to black and Nassau groupers and queen and ocean triggerfish. Turtles visit the upper levels of the reef flat.

## Who You Callin' a Slug?

Among the most beautiful marine animals on the coral reef, nudibranchs have several body shapes, from the dorid form shown here—with two sensory horns up front and a circular gill plume at the rear—to species bearing hundreds of fingerlike projections (cerata) along their backs. The Bay Islands are home to several dozen species of color-

DAVID BEHRENS

ful nudibranchs. They feed on sponges and corals, which are abundant in these waters.

Nudibranchs are hermaphroditic, bearing both male and female sex organs. After mating, each member of the pair crawls off to lay a separate egg mass. This strategy has evolved over time to ensure each species' survival.

Pictured is the gold-crowned sea goddess, *Hypselodoris acriba*. This beautiful chromodorid reaches more than 2 inches (50mm) in length. While considered somewhat uncommon, this one was found crawling on the hull of the *Águila*.

## 15 Peter's Place

Named after live-aboard operator Peter Hughes, who lived on Roatán early in his career, this is a great drift dive. Your dive-master will lead you from the mooring to a cavelike crevice about 70ft down the reef face. You can then drift along the reef crest, which averages about 55ft. Below the crest the wall drops sharply, past the

**Location:** NW of Bailey's Cay

**Depth Range:** 10-130ft+ (3-40m+)

**Access:** Boat

**Expertise Rating:** Novice

sport-diving limit, as it does along the entire north shore.

Turtles are common daytime visitors to the reef, as are large schools of school-masters, blue tangs and Caesar grunts. Yellowtail snappers will follow you around. Solitary barracuda cruise the reef crest, as do coneys, graysbies, tiger groupers and pairs of queen and gray angelfish. Along the wall you'll find schools of horse-eye and black jacks, blue runners and spadefish.

Peter's Place is also a good night dive, easily accessible from the nearby Sandy Bay resorts. After dusk slipper lobsters and hundreds of red night shrimp crawl from their daytime lairs, their eyes glowing under the beam of your dive light. The ruby brittle star sometimes clambers up the blades of sea fans.

## 16 Bear's Den

Bear's Den gets its name from a large underwater cave and volcanic tunnel. Squirrelfish, basslets, hamlets and parrotfish frequent this site, as do various grouper species. You'll also find a variety of black corals.

As you head down the mooring to the reef crest, you'll notice the tunnel entrance. About 100ft long, the tunnel opens onto a steep drop-off in 80ft of water. Sea fans, sea whips and giant vase sponges carpet the tunnel walls, sheltering many reef fish species.

To reach the cave, swim about five minutes east of the mooring. Your dive-

**Location:** West of Sandy Bay

**Depth Range:** 30-105ft (9-32m)

**Access:** Boat

**Expertise Rating:** Intermediate

master will help you find the entrance, which is down around 40ft. The large circular cave will accommodate several divers at a time. Bring a dive light to spot several large channel clinging crabs and lobsters.

The cave is home to long-legged channel clinging crabs.

## 17 Spooky Channel

Accessible by boat or from shore, Spooky Channel is directly off the end of the Sunnyside pier, just east of Bay Islands Beach Resort. Two buoys mark the inner reef—one warns boats away from the shallows, while the other marks the channel entrance. There's also a mooring on the outer reef for those wanting to enter from seaward.

**Location:** Sandy Bay, off Bay Islands Beach Resort

**Depth Range:** 5-95ft (2-29m)

**Access:** Boat or shore

**Expertise Rating:** Intermediate

The channel is a huge cavelike hollow that bottoms out at about 95ft. At the surface the reef is open by only a few feet, forming a nearly complete ceiling. As its name implies, the site is rather dark, though the view into the deep blue offshore water is spectacular. Visibility depends upon the currents, as water moving through the channel does stir up sediment. Stay close to your buddy and carry a dive light.

Although the absence of light limits the abundance of marine life in the chasm, lobsters, octopuses and shrimp are active along its upper reaches, particularly at night. You'll have better luck just outside the channel, where you'll find schools of parrotfish, creole wrasses, barracuda and an occasional grouper or turtle.

## 18 Barry's Reef

Barry's Reef is a typical north shore wall dive. The mooring is in 25ft of water. From there the reef slopes gently seaward to the top of the wall, which drops sharply to a sand bottom at about 80ft.

**Location:** North of Sandy Bay

**Depth Range:** 25-80ft (8-24m)

**Access:** Boat

**Expertise Rating:** Novice

DAVID BEHRENS

A yellowline arrow crab rests in a sponge.

The reef face is broken with numerous fissures and canyons that shelter a variety of invertebrate life. Azure vase sponges will quickly catch your eye. Also abundant is the ubiquitous yellow-and-purple branching tube sponge, *Pseudoceratina*, and its close relative the yellow tube sponge, *Aplysina*. Zoanthids inhabit the sponge surfaces, giving them a spotted appearance, while the sponge openings are favorite hiding places for the yellowline arrow crab, peppermint cleaning shrimp and snapping shrimp. Look closely to find porcelain crabs.

Resident fish life includes queen and stoplight parrotfish and indigo hamlets, which forage alongside several species of damselfish, including the dusky, longfin and threespot. Schools of surgeonfish and wrasses cruise the upper reef flat, and curious barracuda sometimes follow divers. In the spring, ocean triggerfish nest along the bottom of the wall beside the sand flat.

## South Side

Roatán's south side is somewhat remote, its shoreline spotted with a few upscale homes and a number of small shrimping facilities. This remoteness means its reefs are less visited than spots closer to the resorts, thus free of damage from both deleterious shore activity and diver traffic. In one harbor two derelict ships that ran aground years ago offer good snorkeling but are difficult to access.

These sites are most often dived by operators between Coxen Hole, named for a famous British pirate, and French Harbour, home to two of the island's largest dive resorts. Once the center of the banana trade, Coxen Hole is an active, lively town with a supermarket, shops and street vendors. Banana and plantain traders still tie up their *cayucas* (dugout canoes) along the quay.

French Cay and French Harbour are on peninsulas that jut into the sea. Crowding the harbors are shrimp and lobster boats, fishing trawlers and freighters carrying goods between the islands, Central America and the United States. On nondiving days you can tour the harbors and fish-packing plants, and be sure not to miss the more than 2,000 iguanas at the Arch family iguana farm.

DAVID BEHRENS

French Harbour boasts a large fishing fleet.

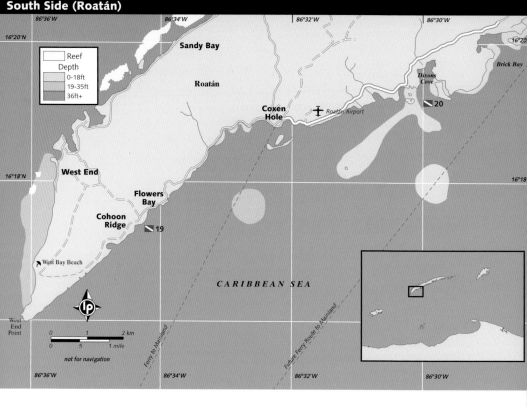

## South Side Dive Sites

| | Good Snorkeling | Novice | Intermediate | Advanced |
|---|---|---|---|---|
| **19** Church Reef & Flowers Bay Wall | | | ● | |
| **20** Insidious Reef | | | ● | |

## 19 Church Reef & Flowers Bay Wall

While they are outside the marine reserve, Church Reef and Flowers Bay Wall are far enough off the beaten track to remain relatively pristine sites. Access is primarily by live-aboard or private yacht, though resort operators will take you here upon request.

Topography is typical of the region, with a reef flat at about 25ft that drops sharply below 130ft. In a current, these make great drift dives. When currents are absent, swim a circular route from the mooring out to the wall and descend to your preferred depth.

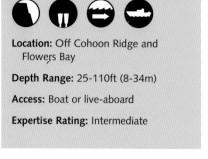

**Location:** Off Cohoon Ridge and Flowers Bay

**Depth Range:** 25-110ft (8-34m)

**Access:** Boat or live-aboard

**Expertise Rating:** Intermediate

Follow the wall left or right and return to the mooring.

Both sites are rich in hard- and soft-coral species. Large heads of pillar coral are common. The reef is broken by sand channels and ridges densely covered with soft-coral species, including 6ft sea plumes and large, colorful sea fans. Often in pairs, flamingo tongues graze on virtually every gorgonian. You'll find plenty of lobsters in the reef crevices, while large schools of jacks, spadefish, cubera snappers and barracuda swim just off the face. The sites have become havens for sea turtles, spotted eagle rays and other species easily displaced by too much activity.

MICHAEL LAWRENCE

Diver hovers over a mature colony of pillar coral.

## 20 | Insidious Reef

Insidious Reef is on a gently sloping off-shore bank just off the fringing reef. The reef crest lies in about 30ft of water and is dominated by fire and pillar corals. The south wall drops below 130ft.

The reef supports a diverse assemblage of marine species. Soft corals and sponges predominate, offering refuge to dozens of fish and invertebrate species. Groupers and sea bass are common, along with blue, midnight and rainbow parrotfish. This dive is an

**Location:** Outside Dixon's Cove

**Depth Range:** 30-130ft+ (9-40m+)

**Access:** Boat

**Expertise Rating:** Intermediate

especially good place to practice your damselfish taxonomy, as you'll find grazing brown chromis, longfin dam-

MICHAEL LAWRENCE

Abundant damselfish include clouds of brown chromis.

selfish, sergeant majors, threespot and yellowtail damselfish. These little guys are extremely territorial and will threaten you with darting advances if you enter their space.

As this site is outside the fringing reef proper, you'll notice greater numbers of pelagic species, including bar jacks, blue runners, black and yellow jacks, horse-eye jacks, permits, sennets and barracuda.

# Central Coast

More than 25 moored dive sites lie along the central coast between Brick Bay Point and Jack Nixon Point. Most are along the seaward edge of the reef face, though there's a great ship and airplane wreck dive in the channel just off CoCo View Resort. This section of the island is also home to the most famous dive site in the Bay Islands—Mary's Place. As almost every dive operator on the island visits Mary's, access is regulated to protect and preserve this beautiful site.

East of French Harbour the shore is less populated and towns are few. The coastline is broken by a series of bights, including First Bight, and Second Bight, which is home port to the islands' only live-aboard, the *Bay Islands Aggressor IV*.

GREG JOHNSTON

Several dive sites lie just offshore from CoCo View Resort.

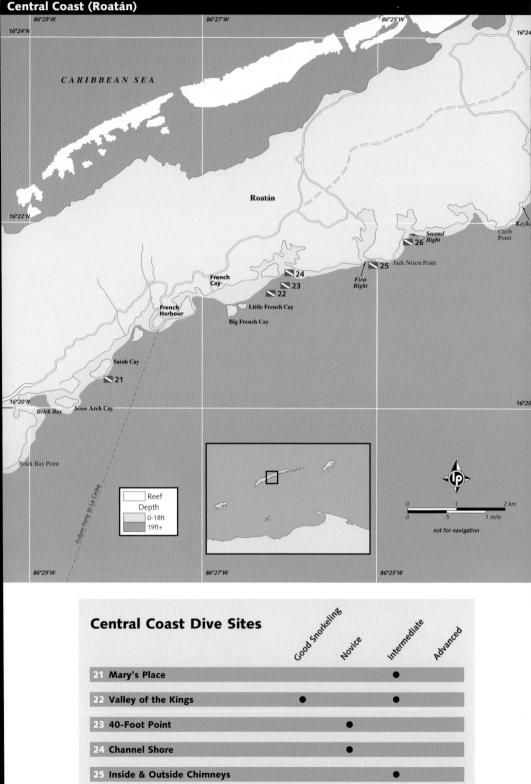

# Central Coast (Roatán)

CARIBBEAN SEA

Roatán

French Cay

French Harbour

Little French Cay

Big French Cay

Sarah Cay

Jesse Arch Cay

Brick Bay

Brick Bay Point

Future Ferry to La Ceiba

First Bight

Second Bight

Jack Nixon Point

Carib Point

Keyh...

21

22

23

24

25

26

Reef
Depth
0-18ft
19ft+

not for navigation

0    1    2 km
0    .5    1 mile

## Central Coast Dive Sites

| | | Good Snorkeling | Novice | Intermediate | Advanced |
|---|---|---|---|---|---|
| 21 | Mary's Place | | | ● | |
| 22 | Valley of the Kings | ● | | ● | |
| 23 | 40-Foot Point | | ● | | |
| 24 | Channel Shore | | ● | | |
| 25 | Inside & Outside Chimneys | | | ● | |
| 26 | Parrot Tree | ● | | ● | |

## 21 | Mary's Place

A visit to Roatán without a dive at this spectacular site is unforgivable. In fact, Mary's Place is so popular that dive operators must schedule time to dive here. The site is named for the wife of a well-known local divemaster.

Sheer-walled vertical faults cut through the reef formation, the result of volcanic activity. From the mooring in about 20ft of water, your divemaster will lead you down one of these two fissures.

The faults descend to about 70ft, meeting about three-quarters of the way to an exit on the reef wall. From here your group may return to the surface through the other fault or continue the dive on the wall, which bottoms out at 110ft. Stay a dozen feet behind the diver in front of you and refrain from touch-

**Location:** Seaward of Sarah Cay

**Depth Range:** 20-110ft (6-40m)

**Access:** Boat

**Expertise Rating:** Intermediate

ing the walls. Most operators also forbid cameras on this dive to assure no rubbernecking within the faults.

Lining the walls are some of the most spectacular black corals on Roatán. At least five distinct species grow in profusion, some reaching 5 to 6ft in height. Look for white, brown, green, red and black varieties. You'll also find huge schools of silversides moving in synch.

MICHAEL LAWRENCE

Huge schools of silversides are common in the crevices of Mary's Place.

## 22 Valley of the Kings

This reef is a great spot for snorkelers and divers alike, as it offers both a shallow reef crest and a wall that drops to the sport-diving limit. It also makes a nice night dive for guests at CoCo View and Fantasy Island Resorts.

Pillar corals and azure vase sponges predominate on the reef, while the site's many overhangs sport large rope sponges and many soft-coral species. You'll find spotted trunkfish, trumpetfish and an occasional toadfish. Look closely at the coral heads and large sponges to spot several goby species.

**Location:** East of Little French Cay

**Depth Range:** 5-130ft+ (2-40m+)

**Access:** Boat

**Expertise Rating:** Intermediate

At night large basket stars spread their treelike limbs from the tops of sea fans. Also watch for reef squid, color-shifting octopuses and clinging crabs, as well as slipper, spiny and spotted lobsters.

## 23 40-Foot Point

One of several moored dive sites off Fantasy Island Resort, this vertical drop-off tops out in 40ft of water, hence the name. Alternate names include **Ventana al Valle** (Window to the Valley) and **Missing Link**.

A variety of fish species congregate in the adjacent channel, which leads to shoreline mangroves. Expect shoals of schoolmasters, yellowtail snappers and Caesar grunts. Other common species

**Location:** Offshore from Fantasy Island Resort

**Depth Range:** 40-130ft+ (12-40m+)

**Access:** Boat

**Expertise Rating:** Novice

include queen and gray angelfish, doctorfish, stoplight parrotfish, lizardfish and large trumpetfish. Various vase and rope sponge species are common here as well, including the pink vase sponge, *Niphastes digitalis*, and the scattered pore rope sponge, *Aplysina fulva*.

At night brittle and basket stars emerge to feed. Keep your eyes open for the fascinating swimming crinoid, which at first looks like a brittle star. Take a closer look and you'll see it has 10 legs and is similar in morphology to its prehistoric relic sessile cousin the black and white crinoid.

DAVID BEHRENS

Unlike a brittle star, the swimming crinoid has 10 legs.

# 24 | Channel Shore

Channel Shore encompasses several dive sites within easy access of CoCo View and Fantasy Island Resorts. This area includes the remains of the **Prince Albert**, a submerged DC-3 airplane fuselage and a steep wall. Currents and boat traffic in the channel often cut visibility, but the dive is worth the tradeoff.

On the east side of the channel is the wall, which leads to a sand flat at 120ft. The *Prince Albert* lies upright in 85ft of water on the west side of the channel. Follow the mooring line to the sand bottom, then swim south—you can't miss her. This 140ft interisland freighter was sunk as an artificial reef in 1987. Her hull is covered with full-grown gorgonians and rope sponges, and the ship's port-

**Location:** Offshore between CoCo View and Fantasy Island Resorts

**Depth Range:** 30-120ft (9-37m)

**Access:** Boat or shore

**Expertise Rating:** Novice

holes and various nooks are perfect habitat for the delicately branched pink *Stylaster* hydrocoral.

A cable leads from the *Prince Albert's* bow to the DC-3. Bring your dive light and take care venturing through the plane. It can be a tight squeeze for some.

## Wreck Diving

Wreck diving can be safe and fascinating. Penetration of wrecks, however, is a skilled specialty and should not be attempted without proper training. Wrecks are often unstable; they can be silty, deep and disorienting. Use an experienced guide to view wrecks and the amazing coral communities that have developed on them.

STEVE ROSENBERG

## 25 Inside & Outside Chimneys

This site is named for two large chimneys, or pinnacles, that rise from about 60ft to within 20ft of the surface. Below the chimneys the wall drops to a sand bottom at 120ft. Currents often sweep the site, supporting such filter-feeding organisms as sponges and gorgonians, as well as various hard corals. These species provide additional substrate and habitat for numerous fish and invertebrate species.

The gorgonians support filter-feeding invertebrates such as winged and frond oysters and several tunicate species. Look for delicate hydroids and bryozoans on the surfaces of these filter feeders, which

**Location:** East of First Bight

**Depth Range:** 20-120ft (6-37m)

**Access:** Boat

**Expertise Rating:** Intermediate

depend on their hosts' natural pumps to draw in nutrient-laden water.

Filefish, pipefish and damselfish forage among the soft corals for minute critters living in the algal turf that grows on any remaining reef substrate.

STEVE ROSENBERG

Currents sweep the chimneys, supporting lush growth.

## 26 Parrot Tree

This is a perfect spot for snorkelers to drift above the reef and explore the many reef crevices. Though sometimes subject to wave action and low visibility, it's also a very good dive for novice and intermediate divers.

**Location:** East shore of Second Bight

**Depth Range:** 5-130ft+ (2-40m+)

**Access:** Boat

**Expertise Rating:** Intermediate

The site comprises two distinct shelves broken by numerous sand chutes. On the reeftop, white scroll, watercress and coralline algae provide good grazing for the spotted sea hare, *Aplysia dactylomela*, the lettuce sea slug, *Elysia crispata*, and other herbivorous mollusks.

This algal turf forms a virtual meadow for herbivorous fish species, including doctorfish, blue tangs and stoplight, queen and rainbow parrotfish. Other less common herbivores found here include redlip blennies, as well as goldspot and bridled gobies. Large schools of sergeant majors and dusky and longfin damselfish forage in the water column above the turf.

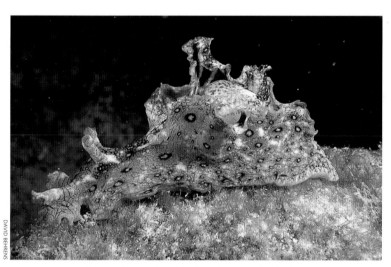

DAVID BEHRENS

A type of mollusk, spotted sea hares reach 6 inches.

# East End

The east end shoreline is composed largely of mangroves. Reached primarily by dive operators around Oak Ridge, its remote sites offer pristine reef habitats that support diverse marine life. From Santa Helena and Rose Cay you're only a hop and a skip from diving Morat Wall and Barbareta.

True water-based fishing villages line the shore from Jonesville to Oak Ridge and Calabash Bight. The main highway now links the towns, but locals still take water taxis to work.

Farther east is Port Royal. The English and Spanish struggled for control of the town for several centuries, and harbor battlement ruins are still evident. Until recently access was only possible by boat, but today the adventurous can drive the

DAVID BEHRENS

Oak Ridge is a typically bustling seafaring town.

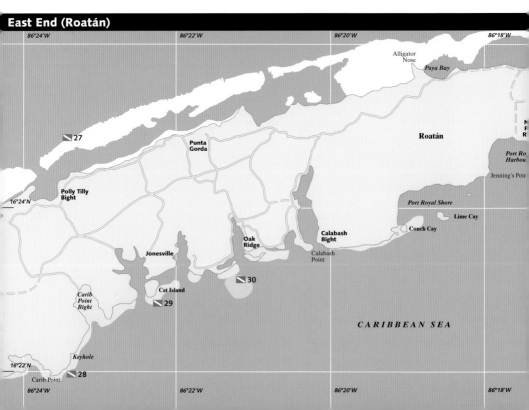

unpaved road into the town. The area boasts beautiful beaches, deep harbors and charming small cays. Several dive resorts visit the great wall dives just offshore.

North of Oak Ridge is Punta Gorda, the oldest settlement on the island. On April 12, 1797, British troops dumped some 3,000 Garífuna (black Caribs) on Roatán following an uprising on the Caribbean island of St. Vincent. While most later migrated to the mainland, a hardy few settled in Punta Gorda and built a new life based on fishing and subsistence farming. Today they maintain many of their traditions, living off the sea and speaking their African dialect. A handful of dive resorts access the north side sites, which are a little farther offshore.

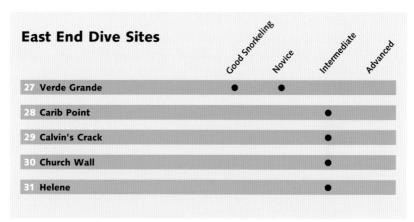

## East End Dive Sites

| | Good Snorkeling | Novice | Intermediate | Advanced |
|---|:---:|:---:|:---:|:---:|
| **27 Verde Grande** | ● | ● | | |
| **28 Carib Point** | | | ● | |
| **29 Calvin's Crack** | | | ● | |
| **30 Church Wall** | | | ● | |
| **31 Helene** | | | ● | |

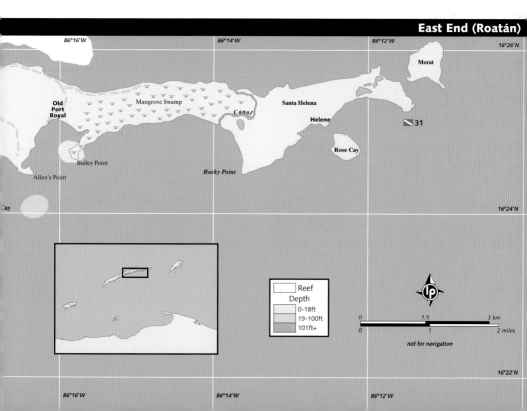

## 27 Verde Grande

This dive is rather removed from other sites along the north shore. Its shallow depth promises good snorkeling for both the nondivers in your group and those who simply can't get enough of the site.

**Location:** West of Punta Gorda

**Depth Range:** 6-40ft (2-12m)

**Access:** Boat

**Expertise Rating:** Novice

Geologically similar to Spooky Channel on Roatán's west end, the site is a system of caverns and cuts through the reef. Dive groups are usually dropped on the outer reef, then picked up on the inner reef after exploring the system of caverns. Bring a dive light for a good look at the resident lobsters, channel clinging crabs and many fish species taking refuge deep inside the labyrinth.

Shallow reefs crests like that at Verde Grande offer terrific opportunities to observe fish behavior up close. Many species will dart in and out of crevices for protection, while others swim confidently ahead of you, scouring the reef for prey. Herbivores in particular seem oblivious to the presence of a curious snorkeler. Parrotfish, wrasses and surgeonfish continue to graze, even reversing direction to swim right beneath you.

## 28 Carib Point

Near both **Keyhole** and **Casablanca** dive sites, Carib Point is a great drift and wall dive. It's not necessary to dive deep

**Location:** Off Carib Point

**Depth Range:** 30-130ft+ (9-40m+)

**Access:** Boat

**Expertise Rating:** Intermediate

DAVID BEHRENS
Giant anemones host spotted cleaner shrimp.

here—just pick a comfortable depth and drift along the reef.

You'll likely see turtles, eagle rays, many grouper species and large schools of jacks. Lush gorgonians and spectacular examples of large barrel and vase sponges grow along the reef face. During your drift, take a moment to inspect the bases of the gorgonians for seahorses and pipefish.

Also near the bases of these soft corals you'll find a variety of sea anemones.

These make great macrophotography subjects. The largest species is the giant anemone, with bulbous purple-tipped tentacles. Several animals associate with this anemone, including spotted cleaner and squat anemone shrimp. Transparent corkscrew and knobby anemones and the bright blue branched anemone are home to Pederson cleaner shrimp. The most curious anemone by far is the hidden anemone. This species wedges its body deep in coral crevices, leaving exposed only the tips of its tentacles, which look like a line of lobster or mantis shrimp eyes peering out from the reef.

## 29 Calvin's Crack

This dive funnels you to the wall through an open tunnel—really a large crack. From the base of the mooring in about 20ft of water, swim toward the wall till you see the crack, which is often full of silversides. The crack descends to 70ft or so, where you exit to the wall.

Rope sponges and black corals are abundant on the reef face. You'll find the red-orange branching sponge, as well as the erect, lavender, row pore and thin rope sponges. Black corals include all color phases of the bushy, feather and orange sea fan black corals. Despite the species' common name, black coral polyps range in color from white to tan, orange, green and black; the namesake black portion of the animal is its hard inner skeleton.

**Location:** South side of Cat Island

**Depth Range:** 20-130ft+ (6-40m+)

**Access:** Boat

**Expertise Rating:** Intermediate

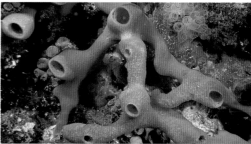
DAVID BEHRENS
Lavender rope sponges crisscross the reef.

## 30 Church Wall

From the base of the mooring in 20ft of water the bottom slopes to the crest of this wall at about 50ft. Soft corals and large sponges are abundant along the slope. The wall drops steeply to almost 200ft. Descend to 90ft or so to find several species of black corals. Various crevices shelter lobsters and clinging crabs.

The wall is also home to several cleaning stations, where peppermint shrimp service a lineup of groupers, triggerfish

**Location:** SW of Oak Ridge Channel

**Depth Range:** 20-130ft+ (6-40m+)

**Access:** Boat

**Expertise Rating:** Intermediate

and snappers. The cleaning stations aren't just for large fish. Many small species, some smaller than the cleaners themselves, stop by to have copepods, isopods and flatworms removed.

Cleaning stations are often manned by several species of cleaners. It's not uncommon to see banded coral shrimp or scarlet-striped shrimp working on a client alongside broadstripe or neon gobies, patiently allowing their mouths and gills to be scoured.

## Taken to the Cleaners

Observant divers will find a variety of symbiotic relationships throughout the marine world—associations in which two dissimilar organisms participate in a mutually beneficial relationship.

One of the most interesting relationships is found at cleaning stations, places where one animal (or symbiont) advertises its grooming services to potential clients with inviting, undulating movements.

Various species of cleaners such as wrasses and shrimp are dedicated to caring for their customers, which may include fish of all sizes and species. Larger fish such as sharks and mantas generally frequent cleaning stations that are serviced by angelfish, butterflyfish and larger wrasses. Turtles generally utilize the services of algae-feeding tangs that are eager to rid them of their algae buildup.

Customers hover in line until their turn comes. When the cleaner attends to a waiting customer—perhaps a grouper, parrotfish or even moray eel—it may enter the customer's mouth to perform dental hygiene, and even exit through the fish's gills. Although the customer could have an easy snack, it would never attempt to swallow the essential cleaner. The large fish benefit from the removal of parasites and dead tissue, while the little wrasses are provided with a meal.

Divers will find that if they carefully approach a cleaning station, they'll be able to get closer to many fish than is normally possible and observe behavior seen nowhere else on the reef.

A grouper awaits the services of two cleaner gobies.

## 31 Helene

Also known as **Rose**, **Santa Helena** or **St. Helene**, this site is very remote and hence infrequently dived, which makes it a tantalizing opportunity. If it's not on your resort's list of regular dive sites, you'll need to use an operator out of Oak Ridge to get here.

Helene boasts a diverse display of habitats and reef life. Fields of sea rods

**Location:** East end of Isla de Santa Helena

**Depth Range:** 20-130ft+ (6-40m+)

**Access:** Boat

**Expertise Rating:** Intermediate

LAURA LOSITO

To stalk prey, fish-eating trumpetfish blend in with the reef.

offer protection to several species adept at mimicking the shape of this soft coral. Most noteworthy is the trumpetfish.

Trumpetfish are piscivores, or fish eaters. This solitary species is able to change its color—usually a gray, brown or yellow—to blend with its surroundings. When hunting, it hovers vertically beside sea rods, head down, waiting to strike unwary passersby. Its expandable trumpetlike mouth enables it to prey on surprisingly large fish.

Trumpetfish also exhibit the curious tactic of sidling up to species such as parrotfish, hogfish and groupers and matching their color, becoming a nearly invisible hitchhiker. When the larger fish feeds, the trumpetfish may benefit from the confusion to strike its own prey. It seems a somewhat unwelcome hitchhiker, however, as parrotfish and groupers will swim erratically and brush against the bottom to shake off the rider.

# Barbareta Dive Sites

Barbareta is an unspoiled, 1,200-acre (485-hectare) privately owned island with numerous worthwhile dive sites. It's been described as mountainous due to its steep rocky shoreline cliffs, which separate isolated sandy beaches. The interior of the island is densely vegetated with ceiba trees and lush rainforest shrubs and is

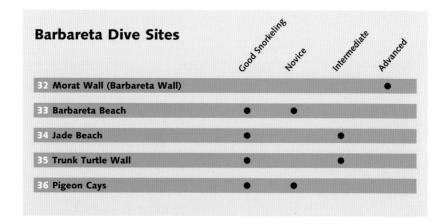

| Barbareta Dive Sites | Good Snorkeling | Novice | Intermediate | Advanced |
|---|---|---|---|---|
| **32 Morat Wall (Barbareta Wall)** | | | | ● |
| **33 Barbareta Beach** | ● | ● | | |
| **34 Jade Beach** | ● | | ● | |
| **35 Trunk Turtle Wall** | ● | | ● | |
| **36 Pigeon Cays** | ● | ● | | |

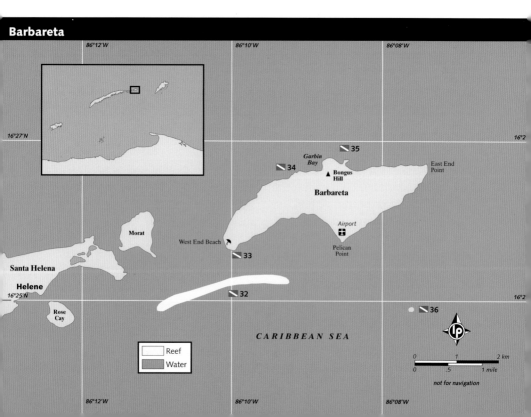

**Barbareta**

home to abundant and diverse Caribbean birds, reptiles and insects. There is one resort on the island, which offers miles of hiking trails, an Amerindian archaeological site and kayaking excursions to the Pigeon Cays and nearby Morat.

Access to Barbareta is by airplane or boat from Roatán. Both the Bay Islands Beach Resort and Anthony's Key Resort offer daytrips to Barbareta. One favorite dive plan begins with a deep dive on Morat Wall, followed by a picnic on the Pigeon Cays, then a final dive at Pelican Point or one of the other shallower sites.

Near West End Beach, Barbareta Beach Club can accommodate 20 guests and provides ecotourism, diving and fishing packages. The resort's Casa Grande villa has five bedrooms and ocean views.

## 32 Morat Wall (Barbareta Wall)

Ask about diving off Barbareta and you'll hear about Morat Wall (also known as Barbareta Wall), one of the most exciting dives in the Bay Islands. The wall stretches almost 3 miles. Exposed to longshore currents, it supports a healthy collection of large filter-feeding sponges. There are no moorings, so divers drift along the face of the wall, a relaxing yet spectacular experience.

**Location:** 1 mile south of West End Beach

**Depth Range:** 40-130ft+ (12-40m+)

**Access:** Boat

**Expertise Rating:** Advanced

Varying in depth from 40 to 70ft, the reef flats support an almost pristine community of elkhorn and staghorn corals, as well as large outcrops of star, brain and plate corals. The vertical wall is broken by numerous canyons and covered with large barrel, vase and rope sponges. Black corals dominate the depths. You'll see colorful schools of yellowtail snappers, schoolmasters, bluestriped grunts, porgies and bar jacks. Keep an eye out for larger pelagics such as eagle rays, barracuda, tarpon and tuna.

STEVE ROSENBERG

Plunging Morat Wall is laden with sponges—and photo ops.

# Get the Drift?

The Bay Islands are known worldwide for their exciting and challenging drift dives. The essential difference between a drift dive and other open-water dives is that you rely on the current to carry you along. Rather than mooring in one place, the dive boat follows your group, picking you up at the end of your dive.

Drift diving can be fun, but divers should be aware of the potential dangers and take extra precautions. The dangers are twofold: being swept away from your group or being injured when a current sweeps you toward a rocky pinnacle or shoreline. Bay Islands dive operators are well accustomed to this type of diving and strive to ensure that you have a safe diving experience. Nevertheless, the following tips will lessen your likelihood of being the subject of a search and rescue mission:

- Drift dives should only be undertaken in calm conditions. Rough seas make you harder to see at the surface should you become separated from the group.

- Divers should always carry sufficient signaling devices, including a marker tube, a signal light and a whistle. The best marker tubes are brightly colored and about 10ft (3m) high. They roll up and easily fit into a BC pocket or clip onto a D-ring. They're inflated orally or with a regulator.

- Always know where your divemaster is.

- Stay with the group. Resist any temptation to wander off on your own, as to do so may take you out of sight of the dive boat.

- Know your skill level. If you're unsure of your ability to undertake any given dive, consult your divemaster.

- Don't do drift dives at night or during twilight. If you get swept away from your group, the darkness will make it much harder for the dive boat to find you.

STEVE ROSENBERG

## 33 Barbareta Beach

Visited regularly by guests from Barbareta Beach Club, this spot offers a shallow sloping beach and all the features of the outer reef. Snorkelers have a diverse collection of corals and fish at their fingertips, while divers enjoy easy access to the nearshore reef.

**Location:** Off West End Beach

**Depth Range:** 5-80ft (2-24m)

**Access:** Boat or shore

**Expertise Rating:** Novice

The reef flat descends to 80ft before dropping into deeper water. Along the slope you'll encounter ridges and heads of star and lettuce corals and some pillar coral. Look closely to spot several species of vase sponges and the yellow-orange variable boring sponge, which invades and breaks down coral heads. Brittle stars, arrow crabs and burrowing zoanthids are common on these sponges. The slope also boasts a variety of gorgonians, which shelter small fish species such as juvenile yellowhead wrasses and scrawled filefish, fairy basslets and harlequin bass.

This is an excellent spot for a night dive. Novice divers and even snorkelers have beach access to shallow areas where they may find elusive basket stars, red night shrimp, spiny lobsters and foraging Caribbean octopuses.

DAVID BEHRENS

Boring sponges secrete an acid to drill into corals.

## 34 Jade Beach

Pieces of jade lie scattered throughout the area, giving this protected site its name. Jade Beach is a wonderful, safe spot for both snorkeling and night diving. A deep crevice splits the reef, offering a more challenging dive.

**Location:** North side near Garbin Bay

**Depth Range:** 20-110ft (6-34m)

**Access:** Boat or shore

**Expertise Rating:** Intermediate

Off the beach a variety of habitats support an array of fish and invertebrates. Along the shallow sand flats you'll see sand tilefish foraging alongside yellow and spotted goatfish. You'll also find large star coral mounds fractured by yellow boring sponges. Hydroids and algal turf fill open spaces between patches of lettuce coral, in turn attracting grazers like clown wrasses and several species of parrotfish. Watch for the occasional hogfish.

Sea fans and sea rods are abundant throughout the site. Among them you'll find mollusks such as flamingo tongues and winged oysters, as well as cryptic fish species such as trumpetfish, triplefins, pipefish and slender filefish.

A parrotfish swims past a star coral mound dotted with boring sponges.

## 35 Trunk Turtle Wall

This is another good spot for both snorkelers and divers, with access to the wall through a channel from the beach. Depending on the time of day, you may encounter slight currents on the wall, enabling you to make this a drift dive.

The wall forms a protective arc that encloses the beach. Carefully inspect the sand corridors within for yellowhead jawfish, stingrays and peacock and channel flounder. Along the wall, even

**Location:** North side off Bongus Hill

**Depth Range:** 20-110ft (6-34m)

**Access:** Boat or shore

**Expertise Rating:** Intermediate

in the shallows, you'll find scorpionfish, spotted morays and an occasional conger eel.

In the shallows be careful to avoid the dense stands of fire coral, both the branching and blade varieties. These will inflict a painful sting on contact, though the rash subsides quickly and will leave no scar.

## 36 Pigeon Cays

You may kayak or boat to this group of three small islands and several sandbars, which offer excellent snorkeling and shallow, easy diving. The sandbars and surrounding turtle grass beds support a variety of interesting species not seen on more exposed reefs, including conchs, sea biscuits, sand dollars, sea stars and rays.

Visitors sometimes spot the upside-down jellyfish, *Cassiopeia*, pulsating rhythmically atop the sand. Its inverted position has significant biological importance to this jelly. Photosynthetic zooxanthellae algae grow in the tissues of its tentacles, and the jelly's orientation toward the sun optimizes the algae's ability to metabolize sugars and

**Location:** 2.5 miles southeast of Pelican Point

**Depth Range:** 25-80ft (8-24m)

**Access:** Boat

**Expertise Rating:** Novice

other byproducts, in turn nourishing its host.

Off the cays, star and brain corals are home to small lobsters and several species of striped gobies. Thick stands of black sea rods wave in the current, and thousands of snapping shrimp produce a chorus of snaps and pops.

DAVID BEHRENS

You'll easily recognize the upside-down jellyfish.

# Guanaja Dive Sites

DAVID BEHRENS

Bayman Bay offers
a nearshore reef and vertical wall.

Sparsely populated Guanaja is the second largest of the Bay Islands. It's reported (though some dispute the claim) that this was the island Christopher Columbus discovered on July 30, 1502, during his fourth and final voyage to the Americas.

Surrounding the island is a dramatic and productive fringing reef, which has been declared a marine reserve from 200ft (60m) deep to the high-tide line. Marine life here is similar to that off Roatán, but Guanaja's patch reefs and small offshore cays offer interesting new habitats for you to explore and enjoy. There are 38 moored sites along the north side and among the cays south of the island. The island's principal settlement, Bonacca, is on one of

| Guanaja Dive Sites | Good Snorkeling | Novice | Intermediate | Advanced |
|---|---|---|---|---|
| 37 The Pinnacle | | | ● | |
| 38 Bayman Bay Drop | ● | ● | | |
| 39 The Pavilions & Michael Rock Channel | | | ● | |
| 40 Volcano Caves (Black Rocks) | ● | ● | | |
| 41 Elkhorn Forest | ● | ● | | |
| 42 Ruthie C | | | ● | |
| 43 Jado Trader | | | ● | |
| 44 Lee's Pleasure | ● | ● | | |
| 45 Jim's Silver Lode | | | ● | |

these small cays. Access between the two sides is via a mid-island canal through the mangroves.

The south side sites are only minutes from shore and feature miles of dramatic coral forests and plunging drop-offs, perfect spots for leisurely drift dives. This side is also home to the wreck of the *Jado Trader*. Reefs along the south side are shallower and interspersed with sand channels.

Be sure to ask your dive operator about other sites not listed here, such as **Vertigo** and the *Don Enrique* wreck. If you visit in winter, don't miss a chance to observe the annual spawning of thousands of groupers at **Caldera del Diablo** (see sidebar, page 82).

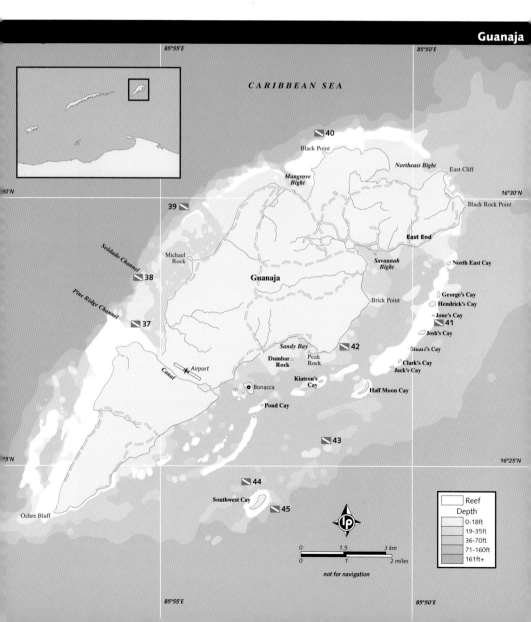

Guanaja

CARIBBEAN SEA

Black Point 40

Northeast Bight  East Cliff

Mangrove Bight

39

Black Rock Point

East End

Soldado Channel

Michael Rock

Savannah Bight  North East Cay

38

Guanaja

Pine Ridge Channel

Brick Point

George's Cay
Hendrick's Cay
Jone's Cay
41

37

Josh's Cay

Sandy Bay  42

Dumbar Rock  Peak Rock

Stuart's Cay

Clark's Cay
Jack's Cay

Canal  Airport

Kiatron's Cay

Bonacca

Half Moon Cay

Pond Cay

43

44

Southwest Cay

45

Ochre Bluff

| | Reef |
| --- | --- |
| | Depth |
| | 0–18ft |
| | 19–35ft |
| | 36–70ft |
| | 71–160ft |
| | 161ft+ |

0   1.5   3 km
0   1   2 miles

not for navigation

## 37 | The Pinnacle

Touted as the best dive on Guanaja, The Pinnacle is at the end of the channel opposite Soldado Beach. It rises from the bottom at 135ft to about 55ft below the surface. Boats moor in about 15ft of water on the reef adjacent to the pinnacle. The ideal dive profile is to descend to between 80 and 90ft, then spiral up the pinnacle to its peak.

From the base of the mooring, swim to the wall, then turn southwest. After a short swim you'll reach the namesake pinnacle. Black corals thrive at depth along its sides. You'll also find a variety of gorgonians, including sea whips, rods and fans, excellent habitat for arrow crabs, flamingo tongues and seahorses.

**Location:** Mouth of Pine Ridge Channel

**Depth Range:** 15-90ft (5-27m)

**Access:** Boat

**Expertise Rating:** Intermediate

Around the pinnacle expect to find groupers, schools of grunts, palometas and barracuda. Basket stars, clinging crabs, slipper lobsters and octopuses are common here at night.

Less than 100 yards to the west are two excellent neighboring sites, **Fantasy Reef** and **Tortuga Reef.**

Look for crinoids amid a carpet of gorgonians.

## 38 Bayman Bay Drop

This is a safe and exciting site for divers of all experience levels. While the highlight is a vertical wall that drops below 180ft, there's also great snorkeling on the reef crest.

**Location:** Mouth of Soldado Channel

**Depth Range:** 10-130ft+ (3-40m+)

**Access:** Boat

**Expertise Rating:** Novice

Along the wall you'll notice an interesting algae, *Dictyota*, which appears to fluoresce bright purple, an even blue under certain lighting conditions. This species is commonly referred to as the Y-branched algae. Photographers often try to capture its iridescence. Several species find this algae tasty, including herbivorous fish and invertebrates such as the lettuce sea slug and spotted sea hare.

The deep reaches are also home to large black coral trees and spectacular tube sponges. In the shallows you'll find a striking assemblage of Caribbean species such as honeycomb cowfish, spotted trunkfish and spotted drums.

DAVID BEHRENS

Lettuce sea slugs feed on the plentiful algae.

## 39 The Pavilions & Michael Rock Channel

These neighboring sites comprise a maze of coral archways, caves and overhangs. Pinnacles and deep crevices provide excellent habitat for lobsters and clinging crabs, and the vertical walls are overgrown with gorgonians. A large anchor and lengths of chain are evidence of an unidentified shipwreck dating back to around 1830. The channel bottoms out at 180ft.

**Location:** North of Michael Rock

**Depth Range:** 35-130ft+ (11-40m+)

**Access:** Boat

**Expertise Rating:** Intermediate

Look closely at the reef substrate to spot the many species of sea anemones and zoanthids that live here. Purple-spotted Pederson cleaner shrimp operate cleaning stations beside almost transparent corkscrew anemones. Other resident anemones include the iridescent blue-green branching anemone, whose tentacles protrude from reef fissures, and the beautiful lavender-tipped giant anemone. Inspect the latter to find commensal spotted cleaner shrimp.

## 40  Volcano Caves (Black Rocks)

Volcano Caves is an ancient lava formation that extends from the seafloor to just below the surface. The lava cooled quickly, forming hundreds of caverns and chambers along the mile and a half long wall. With good planning, it makes a terrific drift dive. Visit this site with an experienced guide.

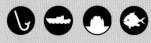

**Location:** North of Black Point

**Depth Range:** 4-65ft (1-20m)

**Access:** Boat

**Expertise Rating:** Novice

Given the geologic history and structure of the caves, don't expect the abundant coral and sponge growth found elsewhere on the island, but the unique lava structures will fascinate you. Many fish species seek refuge in the caves, including schools of silversides and glassy sweepers, as groupers and barracuda patrol the blue water.

### Caldera del Diablo

On the outer reef just east of Guanaja, Caldera del Diablo (Devil's Cauldron) is an underwater canyon that averages 120ft (37m) deep. Though it's a spectacular dive year-round, if you schedule your visit during a full moon in January or February, you'll witness thousands of spawning groupers. Several grouper species choose this lunar cycle to migrate en masse from their usual habitat to propagate. Exactly what draws them to the canyon is unknown.

This is an excellent first dive for the day. The surface interval on your trip back to the island should allow a full day of diving. Due to the site's exposed location, expect surge and currents. This is not a novice dive.

STEVE ROSENBERG

## 41  Elkhorn Forest

Elkhorn Forest is among a series of shallow-water mooring spots along the cays that parallel the southeast coast. Other notable sites include **George's Reef,** **Hector's** and **Windmill Reef.** At each the reef flat is less than 10ft deep, sloping to about 60ft. The clear water and shallow depths offer excellent natural light photo opportunities.

**Location:** Between Jone's and Josh's Cays

**Depth Range:** 2-60ft (1-18m)

**Access:** Boat

**Expertise Rating:** Novice

Snorkelers are able to swim leisurely over shallow reef ridges separated by sand channels and patches, while divers simply pick a direction and make a slow circular swim back to the mooring. The shallow reeftop is home to large schools of damselfish and sergeant majors, as well as the occasional bluehead wrasse, Spanish hogfish and blue parrotfish.

## 42  *Ruthie C*

This submerged shrimp boat sits upright in about 45ft of water only 150ft from the end of the Posada del Sol dock. The hull is covered with a variety of colorful sponges and soft corals. Jacks, angelfish and snappers dart in and out of the vessel's protective remains.

**Location:** Offshore from Posada del Sol resort

**Depth Range:** 35-45ft (11-14m)

**Access:** Boat or shore

**Expertise Rating:** Novice

This shallow nearshore site is a perfect night dive. The cloak of darkness brings out hundreds of feeding shrimp, brittle stars, octopuses and crabs. Ironically, many of the nighttime feeders fall prey to other nocturnal hunters. Octopuses forage for crabs and shrimp, while brittle and basket stars climb atop sea fans and pillar corals to spread their branched arms and capture drifting larvae that rise into the shallows at night.

DAVID BEHRENS

At night giant basket stars fan out their arms to feed.

The resident green moray on the *Jado Trader* expects to be fed.

## 43 Jado Trader

The *Jado Trader* is one of the Bay Islands' most popular dives. The 240ft freighter lies on her port side in 110ft of water on a sand bottom. Beside the wreck is a wall that crests at 45ft. The site is well marked by three buoys. Two of the buoys take you directly to the wreck and the third to **Frisco's Jewel**, a 70ft tall volcanic chimney.

**Location:** NE of Southwest Cay

**Depth Range:** 80-110ft (24-34m)

**Access:** Boat

**Expertise Rating:** Intermediate

The ship was scuttled in July 1987 to create an artificial reef. Its hull boasts a lush growth of sponges and soft corals. Light penetration at the site is so good that algae grow well even at the bottom. Jacks and snappers circle the wreck, while benthic species seek refuge in the crannies of the listing hull.

Visitors to the wreck are often met by a resident green moray, who boldly greets each diver, begging for a tasty handout. Don't be surprised if you find its thick, 6ft-long body threading through your BC or regulator hoses as it looks for a bag of sardines.

## 44 Lee's Pleasure

Lee's Pleasure is one of several great dive sites around Southwest Cay. Sheltered from wind and waves, it's perfect for snorkelers and divers alike. Leeward currents wash the adjoining reefs with nutrient- and plankton-rich waters, providing corals and other marine life with an abundance of food.

**Location:** NW of Southwest Cay

**Depth Range:** 5-70ft (2-21m)

**Access:** Boat

**Expertise Rating:** Novice

The reef slopes down to sand flats at 70ft. A host of sponges and other filter-feeding species make the site spectacularly colorful—a macrophotographer's dream come true. Suggested photo subjects include vase sponges draped with red and gold brittle stars, peppermint shrimp posed in sponge-lined cavities, and spotted cleaner shrimp perched on the purple-tipped tentacles of giant anemones.

This site is an excellent choice for a night dive. As darkness falls, numerous octopuses and clinging crabs come out to forage. Watch for slipper lobsters, as well as large basket stars, which delicately spread their arms into the current to feed.

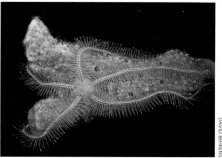

Sponge brittle stars are good climbers.

## 45  Jim's Silver Lode

Jim's Silver Lode is in the same area as **Captain's Crack, Gorgonian Wall** and **Blacktip Slumberland.** These four sites are among the best wall dives in the Bay Islands and are great drift dives when a current is running. The wall gives way to oceanic depths, so there's plenty to see, but keep an eye on your depth gauge and your mind on your dive plan.

After descending the mooring line, swim to the wall and drop to the depth of your choice. At 60ft you'll find the well-advertised tunnel, which you can swim through to a large sandy bowl, home to yellow goatfish, sand tilefish, small stingrays and eyed and channel flounder. You may also encounter almost tame groupers and moray eels, which are used to being fed.

**Location:** SE side of Southwest Cay

**Depth Range:** 50-130ft+ (15-40m+)

**Access:** Boat

**Expertise Rating:** Intermediate

Bring your dive light to explore the many holes along the wall. The face is the perfect place to find and photograph queen triggerfish, black durgon, blackcap basslets, fairy basslets and butterflyfish. Look beneath ledges and in tight crevices to spot several species of squirrelfish and bigeyes, including the longspine squirrelfish and glasseye snapper.

Silversides feed in large clouds atop the wall.

# Cayos Cochinos Dive Sites

The Cayos Cochinos (Hog Islands) are geologically separate from the Bay Islands, lying halfway between the south shore of Roatán and the mainland, about 10 miles (16km) offshore. Clustered within a 5-mile (8km) radius, the group comprises two main islands, Cochino Grande and Cochino Pequeño, and 13 cays of various sizes.

Cochino Grande's mountainous terrain provides good hiking through dense rainforest to a lighthouse, where the view of the surrounding islands is spectacular. The only lodgings, restaurant and bar in the Cayos Cochinos are at Plantation Beach Resort on the island. Although it's principally a dive resort, there are plenty of other activities to keep you busy, including kayaking and snorkeling excursions to Jena's Cove on nearby Cochino Pequeño.

The cays are a treat to dive, boasting a mix of species rare to other Bay Islands. They're also the most difficult islands to visit. The only means of getting to Cochino Grande is by boat. From the mainland there are motorboats out of Nueva Armenia, as well as Marina Laguna, near the Muelle de Cabotaje east of La Ceiba. Anthony's Key Resort on Roatán and Laguna Beach Resort on Utila also offer scheduled trips to the island group, though most local operators and live-aboards will take you there upon request.

JUHA TAMMINEN

Hire a boat to explore one of the pristine outer cays.

The entire island group is protected as a biological marine reserve. Anchoring is prohibited; boats must use established moorings. Most of the 23 nearshore dive sites are off Cochino Grande, while Cochino Pequeño has five moored sites. The surrounding cays are wreathed by a well-developed, pristine fringing reef.

West of the group is a series of seamounts with an additional 11 dive sites— **Bajo Tino, Bajo Tito, Bajo Fiero, Small & Large Morat, Caballero Banks, Mariposa Banks, Dana Bank, Roatán Bank, East Roatán Bank** and **Far East Bank**. They're not described in this book due to their remoteness and level of difficulty. If you're interested in visiting these sites, ask your operator.

## Cayos Cochinos

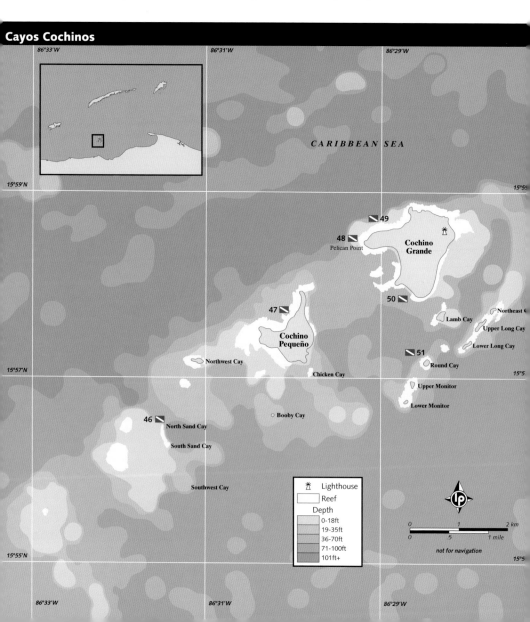

## Cayos Cochinos Dive Sites

| | Good Snorkeling | Novice | Intermediate | Advanced |
|---|:---:|:---:|:---:|:---:|
| **46** North Sand Cay Wall | ● | ● | | |
| **47** Jena's Cove | ● | ● | | |
| **48** Pelican Point Wall | ● | ● | | |
| **49** The Wall | ● | | ● | |
| **50** Thirty-Thirty (Plantation Beach) | ● | ● | | |
| **51** Airplane Wreck | | ● | | |

## 46 North Sand Cay Wall

North Sand Cay has excellent swimming, snorkeling and diving, and its quiet beaches offer a nice spot to relax after your dive. Underwater, a gently sloping shelf drops to depth. The wall is a mix of sand channels and coral ridges.

**Location:** North of North Sand Cay

**Depth Range:** 20-70ft (6-21m)

**Access:** Boat or shore

**Expertise Rating:** Novice

You'll find a wide variety of both hard and soft corals and the usual diverse assemblage of Caribbean sponge species. Peer closely into crevices and beneath overhangs to spot clinging crabs and spiny and spotted lobsters. The ridges are home to numerous cleaning stations, where you'll see banded coral shrimp enticing groupers, angelfish, parrotfish and bass to stop for a grooming. Examine the substrate carefully to discover well-camouflaged frogfish and scorpionfish.

As you progress down the sand channels, you'll come

Deepwater sea fans and sponges grow thick along the wall.

upon large colonies of garden eels. Approach slowly and watch them disappear into their burrows in rhythmic waves. Horse conchs, king helmets and other large mollusk species forage along these sand channels.

## Cayos' Rare Critters

Although difficult to explain biologically, Cayos Cochinos' waters do support a number of species not commonly seen elsewhere in the Bay Islands or, for that matter, elsewhere in the Caribbean. Colonies of purple tunicates are huge here compared to those off the other islands. You may also find the fingerprint cyphoma, as well as the very rare roughback batfish and quillfin blenny (shown at left).

STEVE ROSENBERG

## 47 Jena's Cove

Jena's Cove appeals to divers and snorkelers alike. The cove's gentle sloping bottom, prominent pillars and outer wall support a range of habitats and a diverse collection of fish and invertebrates.

One or more dives here and your Bay Islands marine life checklist will be complete. Studies conducted by the Smithsonian Tropical Research Center documented more than 115 coral species, 195 mollusk species and 45 species of crabs, shrimp and lobsters. Researchers also recorded an amazing 226 fish species.

From shore the bottom slopes to about 35ft, where the wall drops to 70ft.

**Location:** North side of Cochino Pequeño

**Depth Range:** 5-70ft (2-21m)

**Access:** Boat or shore

**Expertise Rating:** Novice

At the foot of the wall, tall vertical pillars form a maze threaded by blue chromis, barred hamlets, blue tangs, French angelfish and thousands of grunts. Slate-pencil urchins wedge into cracks, while octopuses hide in deep crevices.

GRAEME TEAGUE

Vast shoals of tropical species swiftly surround visiting divers here at Cayos Cochinos.

## 48 Pelican Point Wall

This site is perfect for snorkeling, as the reef closely parallels the shoreline. There are lots of large coral heads, primarily elkhorn, staghorn and brain corals. The reef slopes to about 60ft, where the vertical wall drops to 85ft. Thanks to the shallow depths, this is a great site for novice divers and offers wonderful conditions for photography.

**Location:** West end of Cochino Grande

**Depth Range:** 5-85ft (2-26m)

**Access:** Boat or shore

**Expertise Rating:** Novice

Examine the staghorn closely for unique coral predators like the fire worm. You may find this worm wholly engorging branches of the coral. Don't touch it, however, as defensive bristles along the worm's body can inflict a painful sting on the unwary diver. Other worm species found among the coral are colonies of the delicate feather duster worm and hundreds of Christmas tree worms, which can retreat into their tubes in the blink of an eye. To photograph them, approach slowly.

Pelican Point Wall was an important research zone for Smithsonian marine biologists based on Cochino Pequeño in the mid-1990s. Researchers conducted population counts of spiny lobsters and queen conchs and studied seasonal trends in noncommercial species.

## 49 The Wall

This is another site for those who like wall dives and the feeling of nothing below but blue water. The site's east end features ravines and canyons in about 15ft of water. As you swim west, the reef drops sharply to below 130ft. In calm conditions, swim out from the wall and look back for an impressive vista. If a current is running, you'll drift dive the wall.

**Location:** North side of Cochino Grande

**Depth Range:** 15-130ft+ (5-40m+)

**Access:** Boat

**Expertise Rating:** Intermediate

The wall is densely overgrown with rope and tube sponges, large gorgonians and barrel sponges. As you descend, the species composition switches to black corals in several color variations—brown, black, white and green. Keep an eye on the blue to spot passing eagle rays and big barracuda.

In the spring you'll see large queen triggerfish defending their nests against pesky damselfish, who seem to enjoy picking fights with their much larger opponents. The nests are in sand patches and channels near the wall.

The reef face boasts large tube sponges.

## 50 Thirty-Thirty (Plantation Beach)

Just off the resort beach the sloping sand bottom supports large beds of turtle grass. These grassy areas are home to conchs and other sand-dwelling species such as sea stars, sea biscuits and tube worms. The turtle grass also shelters juvenile and herbivorous fish. Watch for balloonfish, pipefish, conger eels and reef squid, which often hover above the grass. The adjoining rocky patches are home to larger fish such as graysbies and hinds.

Past the turtle grass you'll find a number of small tufts of green algae, which are the primary food of several

**Location:** South end of Cochino Grande

**Depth Range:** 5-130ft (2-40m)

**Access:** Boat or shore

**Expertise Rating:** Intermediate

sea slug and sea hare species. The algae vary in shape from martini glass to feather, grape and pinecone shapes. Beyond this point the site slopes into the deep.

# 51 Airplane Wreck

This Cessna twin-engine passenger aircraft lies in about 30ft of water, its fuselage beautifully encrusted with colonies of sponges and tunicates. The artificial reef attracts schools of blue tangs, smallmouth and French grunts, queen and French angelfish, spotfin and foureye butterflyfish and blue chromis.

**Location:** NW of Round Cay

**Depth Range:** 5-30ft (2-9m)

**Access:** Boat

**Expertise Rating:** Novice

Locals say the plane was chartered by the National Geographic Society, which was filming a nature special here. Shortly after taking off from Cochino Grande, the plane crash-landed on the shore of privately owned Round Cay, or Redondo. Although no one was killed in the crash, the film was reportedly damaged beyond repair, and the society decided not to reshoot the special. The plane was later scuttled offshore. How ironic that an airplane carrying photographic evidence of the area's diverse marine life now shelters that same marine life.

GRAEME TEAGUE

Colonial animals coat the fuselage of this scuttled plane wreck.

# Utila Dive Sites

Well west of Roatán and almost the same distance from the mainland, Utila is known by the backpacker set as one of the cheapest places on the planet to get scuba certification. You can find Open Water courses for under US$100 here. Utila also sports the lowest profile of all the Bay Islands—it's possible to see both sunrise and sunset from nearly every point on the island.

Utila's dive sites comprise a series of steep drop-offs along the north shore and about three dozen shallow-water shore and cay dives to the south. The island itself is only 3 miles (5km) wide and 8 miles (13km) long, thus the sites are relatively close together. Divers typically visit a couple of sites a day in one of the three regions that follow.

Reef flats at most sites are shallow, allowing great snorkeling with little or no current. The East End of the island resembles Roatán, with uplifted Pleistocene reef shorelines, while to the southwest is a series of small palm-studded cays. As at sites off Cayos Cochinos, the reefs here boast a high density of coral species, and colonies of purple tunicates are attached to every available holdfast.

## North Side

Dive sites along this side of the island are primarily walls, each with its own character and features. Several of the drop-offs plunge to oceanic depths, with stunning views over the edge into the endless blue.

At 15 to 30ft (5 to 9m) deep, reeftops are fairly shallow. Swim-throughs are common along the edge of the drop-offs, which are laced with crevices, caverns, pinnacles and overhangs of sheet corals. These are spectacular spots from which to watch pelagics cruising the walls.

| North Side Dive Sites | Good Snorkeling | Novice | Intermediate | Advanced |
|---|:---:|:---:|:---:|:---:|
| 52 Ragged Cay, Spotted Point & West End Wall | | | ● | |
| 53 Don Quickset | ● | | ● | |
| 54 CJ's Drop-Off (Old House) | | | ● | |
| 55 Willy's Hole & The Maze | | ● | | |
| 56 The Pinnacle | | ● | | |
| 57 Great Wall (Duppy Water) | | | ● | |
| 58 Blackish Point | | | ● | |

At the heart of the north side is Turtle Harbour, a turtle nesting site. The area has been designated a wildlife refuge and marine reserve to maintain its delicate ecological balance, as has Ragged Cay, a productive rookery for frigate birds and pelicans off West End.

JUHA TAMMINEN

Fishermen clean nets at the end of their workday.

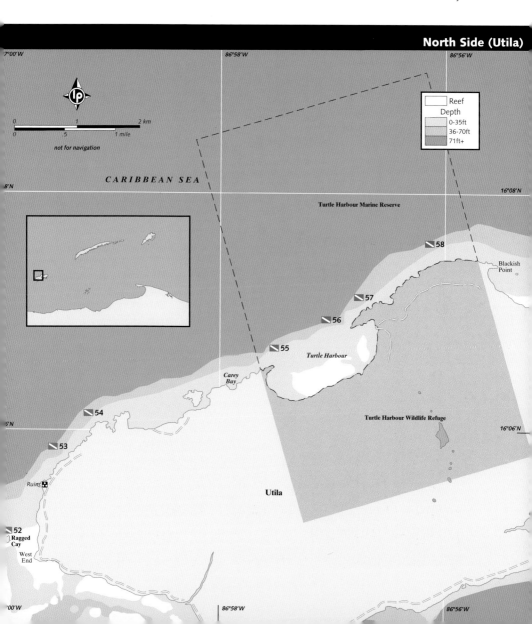

7°00'W

86°58'W

86°56'W

Reef
Depth
0-35ft
36-70ft
71ft+

0        1        2 km
0        .5        1 mile
not for navigation

CARIBBEAN SEA

8'N

16°08'N

Turtle Harbour Marine Reserve

58

Blackish
Point

57

56

55

Turtle Harbour

Carey
Bay

54

Turtle Harbour Wildlife Refuge

5'N

16°06'N

53

Ruins

Utila

52
Ragged
Cay
West
End

'00'W

86°58'W

86°56'W

## 52 Ragged Cay, Spotted Point & West End Wall

These neighboring sites feature shallow reef flats leading to a sheer drop-off that plunges well below the sport-diving limit. When a current is running, this site makes a good drift dive. Monitor your depth gauge to avoid venturing too far down the wall. Most highlights are atop the reef anyway.

**Location:** Off West End

**Depth Range:** 25-130ft+ (8-40m+)

**Access:** Boat

**Expertise Rating:** Intermediate

The sand flats are dotted with large reef patches and coral heads, while the reef crest and wall are thick with both hard and soft corals. Check the many sand channels to find flounder, eagle rays, turtles and, a bit deeper, beds of garden eels. Sit at the edge of the drop-off to watch pelagics passing below.

The sand flats are also home to a number of yellowhead jawfish. This col-

orful species is a great photo subject, but a challenge to capture, as it retreats tail first into its burrow at any sudden movement. Once you've spotted one, sit on the bottom near its hole. When the fish feels safe, it will emerge and hover vertically above its burrow. The males are particularly beautiful.

## A Real Big Mouth

LAURA LOSITO

The jawfish is named for its gaping mouth, which it uses as a shovel to dig its burrow in the sand or coral rubble near a reef. The male jawfish also uses its mouth as an incubator for the female's eggs, a process that lasts five to seven days. If you're lucky, you'll see a proud father-to-be poke his head out from his hole, look around furtively and, when the coast is clear, open his mouth to "churn" the eggs, an action that aerates the clutch and removes waste. When danger threatens—slurp!—into the mouth go the eggs, and down the hole goes the jawfish.

## 53 | Don Quickset

Don Quickset offers amazing topography and variety. Dive with someone who is familiar with the site and can lead you safely back to the mooring.

From the base of the mooring, follow the wall northeast to two canyons that split the reef face. Drop down one of these canyons to a small sand flat at 65ft, then descend to about 70ft to explore a cave surrounded by pinnacles and large coral heads.

A dive light is recommended, and caution should be taken entering the cave. Within the cave you'll find schools of glassy sweepers and an occasional spotted drum. The crevices and cran-

**Location:** Near West End, north of ruins

**Depth Range:** 15-90ft (5-27m)

**Access:** Boat

**Expertise Rating:** Intermediate

nies are also hiding places for octopuses, clinging crabs and lobsters.

At 90ft, the sand bottom is home to lots of sand-dwelling fish and invertebrates. Look closely to find small stingrays and flounder.

DAVID BEHRENS

Octopuses emerge from the caves at night to hunt.

## 54  CJ's Drop-Off (Old House)

This northwest-facing wall drops from a reef flat at 30ft to a sand bottom at about 100ft. After dropping over the edge, swim right or left, depending on the current. The steep wall features ridges, caves and pillar-like outcrops, providing myriad hiding places for fish and lobsters. Monitor your depth carefully.

**Location:** Midway between West End and Carey Bay

**Depth Range:** 30-100ft (9-30m)

**Access:** Boat

**Expertise Rating:** Intermediate

To take in a spectacular panorama, you may want to swim out from the wall and look back at the majestic sheet coral outcrops. Light reflects off the sand bottom, bathing the reef in a tropical blue cast.

At this site you'll find spotted drums, porcupinefish, squirrelfish and grunts. The shallow reef crest is a good place to search for lettuce sea slugs and other nudibranchs. The sunlit portions of the reef are coated with white scroll and watercress algae. You'll find schools of damselfish, wrasses and sergeant majors foraging through this turf.

DAVID BEHRENS

The long finned juvenile spotted drum is a favorite among photographers.

## 55 Willy's Hole & The Maze

While the shallow reeftop is sandy and sparsely populated with soft corals, terrain at this site is spectacular, including caves and canyons, big pinnacles and coral heads. Deeper features are protected from surge and currents, but divers wishing to see the shallows should plan this dive for a calm, clear day.

**Location:** West end of Turtle Harbour

**Depth Range:** 15-130ft+ (5-40m+)

**Access:** Boat

**Expertise Rating:** Novice

Steep spooky walls mark The Maze.

Willy's Hole centers on a group of caves. To reach them, swim down the large crevice from the base of the mooring in 30ft of water. The namesake cavern is at 80ft, and the crevice continues down to a sand bottom at 130ft. Swim east from the mooring to reach The Maze, a series of deep canyons with steep walls.

Goliath groupers, or jewfish, often visit the area, while jacks, snappers and chub circle the reef. Investigate the many holes and cracks for peppermint shrimp, which man cleaning stations, as well as various small anemones, each with its own commensal shrimp. You'll also find lovely clusters of feather duster worms and mats of colorful zoanthids.

## 56 The Pinnacle

The highlight of this dive is a dramatic pinnacle that rises alongside the wall. Divers first follow their divemaster to a swim-through at about 80ft, just west of the mooring. Give each other room as you negotiate this swim-through. You'll exit the wall at about 125ft, then quickly ascend to maximize your bottom time.

**Location:** East end of Turtle Harbour

**Depth Range:** 20-130ft+ (6-40m+)

**Access:** Boat

**Expertise Rating:** Novice

From there swim east, following and crossing the deep channel to find the pinnacle. Circle it to the surface and your safety stop, all the while checking crevices for eels, crabs, lobsters, nudibranchs, squirrelfish, drums and several blenny species.

West of the pinnacle the wall drops to deeper water. To the east, at about 60ft, is a series of sand channels and large coral outcrops. Black durgon, scrawled filefish and foureye and spotfin butterflyfish patrol the sand/reef perimeter for algae and small prey.

## 57 Great Wall (Duppy Water)

This is one of the best sites along the wall off Turtle Harbour, a truly breathtaking oceanic drop-off. The mooring is in 30ft near the crest of the wall. Just behind the buttress is a sand patch at about 50ft, a good starting point for novice divers. "Duppy" means ghost in West Indian, and it's said that ghosts will try to draw you ever deeper on this wall. Watch your gauges and stick to your dive profile.

**Location:** East end of Turtle Harbour

**Depth Range:** 25-130ft+ (8-40m+)

**Access:** Boat

**Expertise Rating:** Intermediate

Drop down between 80 and 90ft to find huge barrel sponges, many gorgonians and black corals. If you have enough bottom time, there's more to see just below 100ft. Follow the wall to the west until you find a sand channel at 50ft that will take you back to the mooring.

This site is frequented by any number of pelagics and is home to rays, flounder and yellowhead jawfish. While enjoying the bottom-dwelling critters, glance up periodically to spot large tarpon and barracuda.

This magnificent wall boasts towering barrel sponges and lots of schooling fish.

## 58 Blackish Point

Blackish Point offers a north-facing wall with many crevices and caves. The sheer face drops to a sand bottom at 80ft, which at certain times reflects the sunlight, tinting the wall a deep blue. This site experiences strong currents, so use discretion when planning your dive. Consider a drift dive to see more of the unique topography.

**Location:** West of Blackish Point

**Depth Range:** 30-80ft (9-24m)

**Access:** Boat

**Expertise Rating:** Intermediate

MICHAEL BEHRENS

Creole wrasses hover nose down, possibly to attract cleaners.

Pick a direction and descend to about 60 or 65ft. In the absence of a current, you can head either way. Some divers claim there are more fish to the west, but both sides shelter several species of parrotfish, butterflyfish and surgeonfish, as well as schools of silversides, French grunts and creole wrasses.

The latter species often hovers in a peculiar vertical swimming position. Originally thought to be some form of spawning behavior, recent research suggests the wrasse assumes this position to attract the attentions of helpful cleaner fish.

## East End Dive Sites

| | Good Snorkeling | Novice | Intermediate | Advanced |
|---|---|---|---|---|
| **59 East End Reef (The Aquarium)** | ● | ● | | |
| **60 Black Hills** | | | ● | |
| **61 Ted's Point** | | | ● | |
| **62 Airport Reef (Airport Caves)** | ● | | ● | |
| **63 Ron's Wreck** | | ● | | |
| **64 *Halliburton*** | | | ● | |
| **65 Lighthouse Reef** | ● | ● | | |
| **66 Utila Lodge** | ● | ● | | |

# East End

Visited by all of Utila's dive operators and resorts, the East End sites are a short run from the town of Utila (also called El Centro) and even Laguna Beach Resort. A typical day might start with an East End dive followed by a north side dive.

The land along East End Point is composed of uplifted Pleistocene coral reef. Accessible only by boat, the waters here are known for whale shark and other pelagic encounters. Dive boats share information on whale shark sightings by radio.

Dive sites close to the airport are off sandy beaches more typical of the island. These sites are a good choice for divers staying in town or desiring shore dives. They also offer excellent shallow-water night diving.

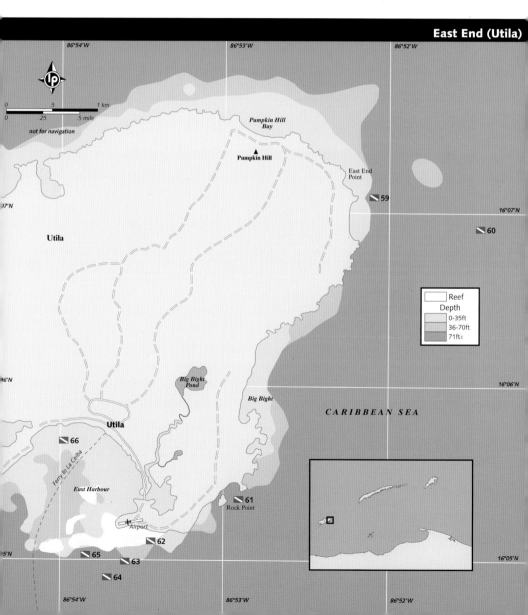

## 59 East End Reef (The Aquarium)

Depending on currents, East End Reef can be a great snorkeling spot or a terrific drift dive. Pick your depth along the gradual slope and hover as close to the reef as you'd like. This opportunity for close-up observation is why some operators refer to the site as The Aquarium.

**Location:** Just off East End Point

**Depth Range:** 5-60ft (2-18m)

**Access:** Boat

**Expertise Rating:** Novice

Volcanic and Pleistocene geologic activity formed a maze of arches and interesting shapes along the edge of the wall, while on the upper reef slope, stretches of sand alternate with large coral patches. These coral patches support a variety of gorgonians, including *Plexaura* sea rods, *Eunicea* candelabrum and *Pterogorgia* sea whips. The area also boasts a variety of sea fans and large branching sea plumes. Look closely on these species to find flamingo tongues and winged oysters. You may also spot seahorses, which hover at the base of these gorgonians.

JUHA TAMMINEN

Volcanic and geologic forces spawned the startling reef formations.

## Northeastern Pelagics

About a mile or so off East End Point, Northeastern Pelagics is a blue-water dive for those hoping to see large pelagic species. When conditions are right you may spot whale sharks, mantas, marlins, sailfish and schools of bonitos, as well as several shark species. This is an advanced dive, and caution is suggested due to variable currents and surge. Buoyancy control is the name of game here, as there are no visual references by which to gauge your depth. Make sure you're comfortable with using your BC before attempting this dive.

SCOTT TUASON

## 60 Black Hills

When conditions are right, this is one of the best dives on Utila. There's no mooring, so you'll be dropped directly above this seamount, which rises from 130ft to within 40ft of the surface. Descend to about 80ft, then circle the mount back to the top. If a current is running, your operator should drag a drift line behind the boat.

You'll see schooling jacks, barracuda, chub, spadefish and several species of triggerfish. This is also a favorite gather-

**Location:** Offshore from East End Point

**Depth Range:** 40-80ft (24-40m)

**Access:** Boat

**Expertise Rating:** Intermediate

ing spot for pelagics, particularly whale sharks. Wide-angle photo opportunities abound, as visibility is often very good.

## 61 Ted's Point

West of the mooring the bottom varies in depth from 25 to 50ft. A number of chutes slope to a large coral head beside a sand flat at 60ft, home to a large population of garden eels. Other bottom-dwelling species common here are peacock flounder, stingrays and sailfin blennies. East of the mooring the wall drops well below 130ft.

As you follow the wall, explore the many reef crevices to find all forms of nudibranchs, which feed on sponges, and commensal shrimp, which man cleaning

**Location:** NE of airport

**Depth Range:** 40-130ft+ (12-40m+)

**Access:** Boat

**Expertise Rating:** Intermediate

stations. Watch these shrimp dance to entice the next fish in line, which may roll on its side, allowing the shrimp access to its mouth, gills and flanks.

## 62 Airport Reef (Airport Caves)

Nearshore currents sweep this site, so time your dive carefully. The wall is

**Location:** SE of airport

**Depth Range:** 7-75ft (2-23m)

**Access:** Boat or shore

**Expertise Rating:** Novice

JUHA TAMMINEN

Close to shore, the caves offer several interesting swim-throughs.

pocked with crevices and three large caverns between 20 and 40ft. To find the caverns, either follow an experienced dive guide or, if you're on your own, make a few short sweeps along the shore till you find them.

Travelers staying in town can walk to the airport and cross its gravel runway to snorkel this wonderful reef. The shallows support lush staghorn and elkhorn corals. Look along the tips of staghorn branches to spot feeding fire worms. One has to wonder how the worm can wholly swallow this jagged hard coral.

When conditions allow, this is also an excellent night dive. Darkness brings out curious lobsters, clinging crabs, shrimp, numerous eels, spotted eagle rays, nurse sharks and other nocturnal species.

## 63 Ron's Wreck

Sunk as an artificial reef in 1991, this 35ft boat provides a safe shallow dive. Lying in 45ft of water, the hull is beautifully colonized with sponges, hydrocorals, bryozoans, tunicates and numerous species of soft corals.

Just north of the wreck is a large sand patch surrounded by a low reef wall. Known among local divemasters as

**Location:** South of airport

**Depth Range:** 45-90ft (14-27m)

**Access:** Boat

**Expertise Rating:** Novice

**Moonpool**, this is a great spot for a night dive. The substrate is crawling with species you rarely see in daylight, including red night shrimp, lobsters and channel clinging crabs, which clamber out on sea fans. You'll be able to closely approach squirrelfish and sleeping parrotfish.

Microscopic plankton put on a magical display of bioluminescence at night. Simply turn off your dive light, or point it into your chest, and the water comes alive with wiggling, jerking green lights. The natural light produced by these marine organisms is their own tiny version of a dive light.

## 64 Halliburton

The *Halliburton* was sunk as an artificial reef on May 4, 1998. The 210ft ship rests upright in a sand channel and slopes from 60 to 100ft. For biologists and underwater photographers, exploring a wreck like the *Halliburton* is like browsing through a supermarket.

Artificial reefs increase the available living space for a variety of encrusting

**Location:** Offshore south of airport

**Depth Range:** 60-100ft (18-30m)

**Access:** Boat

**Expertise Rating:** Intermediate

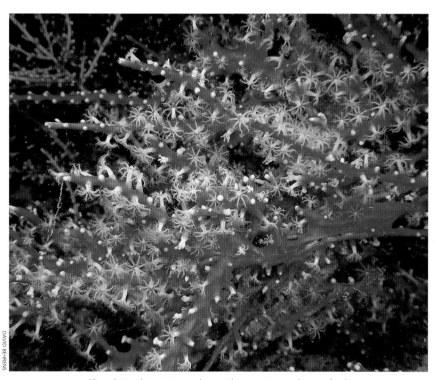

DAVID BEHRENS

The white telesto octocoral extends its cottony polyps to feed.

animals. Numerous overhangs and holes in the ship harbor lovely pink and purple lace corals and shade-loving species like *Tubastraea* cup corals, while masts and crane davits are encrusted with purple tunicates and sponges of every description. This is also a rare opportunity for underwater photographers to capture the polyps of white telesto octocorals on film.

Bring along a dive light to investigate the inner hull, where you'll find spiny lobsters and octopuses, as well as schools of damselfish, squirrelfish and an occasional grouper. Look carefully in the tight crevices to spot snapping shrimp, which produce their near-constant signature sound with a large specialized claw, or cheliped—much like we snap our fingers.

## 65  Lighthouse Reef

A shallow reef that parallels the airport runway, Lighthouse is a good snorkeling site and beginner dive, offering a range of habitats and marine life typical of Utila. It's also a fantastic night dive. The site has three distinct regions: the shallow reeftop, where sand patches separate multiple coral heads; a series of sand

**Location:** Off point west of airport

**Depth Range:** 10-60ft (3-18m)

**Access:** Boat

**Expertise Rating:** Novice

MICHAEL BEHRENS

A pair of camouflaged lizardfish lies motionless atop the sand.

channels that cut the reef wall; and finally, the sand bottom at about 60ft.

You'll spot yellow stingrays, goatfish, jawfish and lizardfish in the sandy shallows, rays and flounder in the sand channels, and several large coral outcrops in deeper water. Other common species include spotted trunkfish, balloonfish, trumpetfish, yellowhead and bluehead wrasses, barred hamlets, cocoa damselfish and schools of blue tangs. You'll also find most of Utila's sponge species plus gorgonians, sea fans and sea whips.

## 66 Utila Lodge

The house reef at Utila Lodge offers terrific snorkeling. A short swim past the turtle grass beds are patch reefs in only 10ft of water. Schools of snappers, grunts, goatfish and parrotfish forage among the gorgonian-covered coral heads, and the surrounding sand is home to conchs, sea biscuits and other

**Location:** Offshore from Utila Lodge

**Depth Range:** 10-35ft (3-11m)

**Access:** Shore

**Expertise Rating:** Novice

Among the most striking marine species, reef squid seem lit from within.

shallow-water species. Flamingo tongue snails graze on sea fans, purple cleaner shrimp wait for customers near beaded anemones, and schools of squid watch you cautiously from a distance.

Because of its proximity to the beach, this is also a great spot for night diving and snorkeling. As darkness falls, Spanish lobsters and king helmet snails emerge from the sand to forage. Squid are also present, hovering just out of reach as they feed on planktonic species. Flash your light at them to observe their rapid color changes.

# South Side

DAVID BEHRENS

Laguna Beach is the jumping-off point for several dive sites.

The south side features a number of relatively shallow dive sites, many great for snorkeling. Nearshore reefs and a series of small cays to the southwest offer much different diving than that found along the north side's plunging drop-offs. Slightly offshore to the southeast are a series of seamounts, offering another dimension to Utila's diving opportunities. Between Laguna Beach and Silver Gardens several dive boats often moor in a row, speaking to the area's popularity among divers.

## South Side Dive Sites

| | Good Snorkeling | Novice | Intermediate | Advanced |
|---|---|---|---|---|
| 67 Laguna Beach & Laguna Bank | ● | | ● | |
| 68 Black Coral Wall & Silver Gardens | ● | | ● | |
| 69 Pretty Bush | ● | ● | | |
| 70 Little Little Bight & Little Bight | ● | ● | | |
| 71 Jack Neil Point | ● | | ● | |
| 72 Big Rock | | ● | | |
| 73 Cabañas | | | ● | |
| 74 Stingray Point | | | ● | |

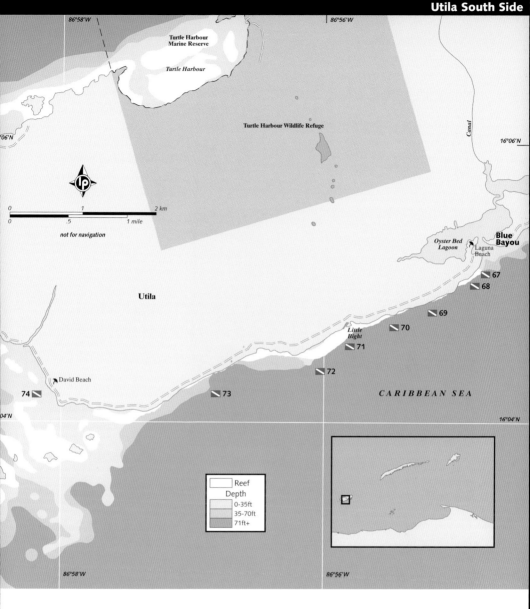

86°58'W · 86°56'W

Turtle Harbour
Marine Reserve

Turtle Harbour

Turtle Harbour Wildlife Refuge

16°06'N

Canal

0    1    2 km
0    .5    1 mile

not for navigation

Oyster Bed
Lagoon

Laguna
Beach

**Blue
Bayou**

67
68

Utila

69

70

*Little
Bight*

71

72

David Beach

*CARIBBEAN SEA*

74

73

16°04'N

86°58'W · 86°56'W

| Reef |
| Depth |
| 0-35ft |
| 35-70ft |
| 71ft+ |

## 67   Laguna Beach & Laguna Bank

Across the channel from **Blue Bayou**, another good area site, Laguna Beach promises an easy shore entry for both snorkelers and divers. Lining the beach are many conveniences, including a local restaurant.

Snorkelers will enjoy looking for conchs, sea biscuits and puffers that hide in the turtle grass near shore. At certain

**Location:** Offshore from Laguna Beach Resort

**Depth Range:** Surface-100ft (30m)

**Access:** Boat or shore

**Expertise Rating:** Intermediate

times of the year you'll spot the upside-down jellyfish, which pulsates rhythmically toward the bottom. It's fun to watch this harmless jelly on its seemingly endless attempt to burrow to China.

Just offshore the wall drops from 15 to 100ft. The face supports lovely colonies of purple tunicates and black and white crinoids, as well as flying gurnards, stargazers and checkered puffers.

Accessible only by boat, Laguna Bank is about half a mile south of Laguna Beach. This shallow-water site is home to diver-friendly green moray eels, as well as several hawksbill turtles. Bring your camera.

Both sites offer habitat for cruising eagle rays, stingrays, yellow-head jawfish, several eel species, sennets, checkered puffers, octopuses, nudibranchs and various species of anemones with resident commensal shrimp. The channel between the sites is home to a large orange longlure frogfish. Night diving is popular at both sites.

DAVID BEHRENS

Snorkelers may spot queen conchs—and vice versa.

## 68 Black Coral Wall & Silver Gardens

There is beach access to Black Coral Wall, which drops precipitously just west of the boat mooring. As its name implies, this sheer nearshore wall is an excellent spot to find black corals, as well as deepwater gorgonians. The site is also home to eels, toadfish and drums.

Silver Gardens is just west of the wall. Though access is by boat, this is also a great snorkeling site, boasting a wide variety of soft and hard corals. Black corals are common here too. The mooring is in 20ft of water in a section dominated by large elkhorn corals, which form a protective thicket for blue and brown chromis. Smallmouth

**Location:** Just SW of Laguna Beach

**Depth Range:** 20-130ft+ (6-40m+)

**Access:** Boat or shore

**Expertise Rating:** intermediate

grunts also retreat here when threatened.

Underwater photographers will appreciate Silver Gardens. The shallow, sunlit depths promise good wide-angle photo opportunities. Even beginners should have some success with a disposable point-and-shoot camera.

JUHA TAMMINEN

A trumpetfish tries and fails to blend into the reef at Silver Gardens.

## 69 Pretty Bush

Typical of area reefs, Pretty Bush is a shallow dive spot with a gentle slope that offers plenty for divers and snorkelers to enjoy. The mooring is in 25ft near the reef crest. From the mooring swim east, descending the slope to explore the terraces and crevices. You'll soon reach the bottom of a sand slide, where you'll find a variety of rays, flounder and sand-dwelling invertebrates.

The site features an exciting swim-through that you can use to ascend or descend the reef face. In the swim-

**Location:** .5 mile (.8km) west of Laguna Beach

**Depth Range:** 25-75ft (8-23m)

**Access:** Boat or shore

**Expertise Rating:** Novice

through you'll encounter such shade-loving species as stinging hydroids, black corals and several colonial tunicate species. These species are also favorite foods of several nudibranch species, so have a close look. Barracuda, cubera snappers, butterflyfish, angelfish, cornetfish and puffers frequent the site.

Translucent tunicates, or sea squirts, are colonial filter feeders.

## 70  Little Little Bight & Little Bight

Blurring into one another, these adjacent sites are yet another option for both snorkelers and divers. From shore the seascape changes from sand to a gentle reef face, then the sand bottom and scattered coral heads at 70ft. Snorkelers can explore offshore to the depth of their choice, while divers should drop to the bottom of the slope and work their way back up to the beach.

Boats moor in about 20ft of water close to the reef face. Descend to the bottom of the slope at about 50ft. From here swim across the sand to any of several coral outcrops in 70ft of water, where you'll find black corals, purple

**Location:** 1 mile (1.6km) west of Laguna Beach

**Depth Range:** Surface-70ft (21m)

**Access:** Boat or shore

**Expertise Rating:** Novice

tunicates and black and white crinoids. Watch for a colony of garden eels hovering atop the sand.

While these are perfect last dives of the day, both also make superb night dives. Shine your dive light into the reef crevices to spot numerous shrimp species, including snapping shrimp.

# 71 Jack Neil Point

This site and its namesake point were named for a notorious local pirate who used sheltered Oyster Bed Lagoon as a hideaway between raids along the coastline in the late 1700s.

Along the gentle reef slope is a steep ledge with several deep cuts that drop to about 40ft. These cuts and their overhangs are draped with rope sponges and gorgonians. A series of coral outcrops at the base of the slope provide habitat for lobsters, channel crabs and various shrimp. Beginning at 60ft, the sand bottom is home to stingrays, halibut and hundreds of elusive garden eels.

**Location:** 1.5 miles (2.4km) SW of Laguna Beach

**Depth Range:** 5-100ft (2-30m)

**Access:** Boat

**Expertise Rating:** Intermediate

Return to the mooring, pausing to watch schools of blue tangs and harlequin wrasses that graze among the corals and sponges. Several species of brittle stars, arrow crabs and boring zoanthids associate with the sponges, which provide food to their residents.

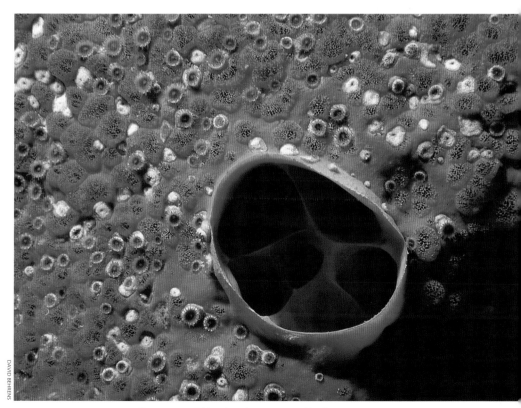

DAVID BEHRENS

Sponge zoanthids set up home on a red boring sponge.

## 72 Big Rock

Among the best dive sites on Utila, this site has two moorings to choose from and offers a range of features. As at neighboring sites, the shallow reef flat drops to a sand bottom at about 80ft.

**Location:** 1.75 miles (2.8km) SW of Laguna Beach

**Depth Range:** 15-80ft (5-24m)

**Access:** Boat

**Expertise Rating:** Novice

The south mooring is in 17ft of water, near a tunnel formed by overlapping sheet corals. Resist the temptation to swim through this tunnel, as you may damage the fragile coral formation. Keep to the right of the tunnel, heading southeast, and you'll reach two coral pinnacles in 35 to 50ft of water. These spires are covered with black corals, sponges and gorgonians. In the surrounding sand you'll find stingrays, channel and peacock flounder and a colony of garden eels. The garden eels alone are worth the price of admission. As you approach, note how they retreat into their holes in unison, one row at a time. To catch a glimpse of them, remain motionless for several minutes.

From the north mooring swim east and drop into the adjacent sand channel. Head south along the bottom of the slope to the pinnacles or swim up and over the sheet coral tunnel near the south mooring.

## 73 Cabañas

STEVE ROSENBERG

Look carefully along the ledges to find spotted scorpionfish.

**Location:** 1.5 miles (2.4km) east of David Beach

**Depth Range:** 25-100ft (8-30m)

**Access:** Boat

**Expertise Rating:** Intermediate

Cabañas features two large pinnacles that rise from 100ft to within 45ft of the surface. Inshore of the pinnacles is a sheer wall of spur-and-groove formations that drop to about 70ft. The site name derives from sheet coral outcrops at the base of the wall that resemble little huts, or cabanas. The reeftop is a maze of sand chutes and patches.

Drop to the bottom and circle each pinnacle, exploring their many shelves to find camouflaged spotted scorpionfish and flamboyant dancing drums. As you meander back toward the reeftop, you'll see foraging triggerfish and large parrotfish, schools of white mullet, young barracuda and French grunts.

## 74 Stingray Point

As the name suggests, stingrays and spotted eagle rays are common visitors to this site. The mooring rests in about 20ft of water. Swim down the wide sand slope directly beneath the mooring to find a colony of garden eels, as well as the occasional lizardfish, southern stingray or peacock flounder.

**Location:** Off of David Beach

**Depth Range:** 20-100ft (6-30m)

**Access:** Boat

**Expertise Rating:** Intermediate

East and west of the sand slope is a steep wall. Just off the east wall you'll find four tabletop coral outcrops that mark the best turnaround point—the first at 50ft and the second at 60ft. Below the outcrops the reef slopes to a sand bottom at 100ft.

The wall and reef flat are thickly populated with sponge and soft-coral species. Careful observers will spot seahorses at the base of gorgonians and flamingo tongue snails grazing on sea fans. The site also supports razorfish, several blenny species, trunkfish, puffers, angelfish and frogfish. Groupers are occasional visitors, as are tarpon and barracuda.

This site is often included on a daytrip to one of the shallow nearby cays such as Morgan's, Pigeon or Jack Neil's, which offer unique opportunities for birdwatching and beachcombing.

STEVE ROSENBERG

Approach stingrays slowly for an up close look at this sand dweller.

DAVID BEHRENS

# Marine Life

Marine life in the Bay Islands spans the spectrum of Caribbean species, carried here by southerly currents that sweep the entire region. Many of the fish and invertebrates derive from the Belize Barrier Reef, northwest of the islands. The diversity of habitats, ranging from steep walls to protected reef flats and shallow mangroves, offers ideal conditions for larval development, as well as robust and sustainable adult populations.

The most noticeable difference between the Caribbean and tropical Indo-Pacific is the overwhelming diversity and abundance of sponge species you'll find in these waters. And while both areas support various hard and soft corals, you'll note clear differences in species composition.

Keep in mind that common names are used freely by most divers and are often inconsistent. The two-part scientific name is more precise. This system is known as binomial nomenclature—the method of using two words (shown in italics) to identify an organism. The first italic word is the genus, into which members of similar species are grouped. The second word, the species, refers to a recognizable group within a genus whose members are capable of interbreeding. Where the species is unknown or not yet named, the genus name is followed by *sp.*

## Common Vertebrates

LAURA LOSITO

squirrelfish
*Holocentrus rufus*

DAVID BEHRENS

trumpetfish
*Aulostomus maculatus*

LAURA LOSITO

graysby
*Cephalopholis cruentata*

STEVE ROSENBERG

black grouper
*Mycteroperca bonaci*

LAURA LOSITO

indigo hamlet
*Hypoplectus indigo*

LAURA LOSITO

fairy basslet
*Gramma loreto*

bar jack
*Caranx ruber*

yellowtail snapper
*Ocyurus chrysurus*

schoolmaster
*Lutjanus apodus*

yellow goatfish
*Mulloidichthys martinicus*

Atlantic spadefish
*Chaetodipterus faber*

foureye butterflyfish
*Chaetondon capistratus*

French angelfish
*Pomacanthus paru*

queen angelfish
*Holacanthus ciliaris*

creole wrasse
*Clepticus parrai*

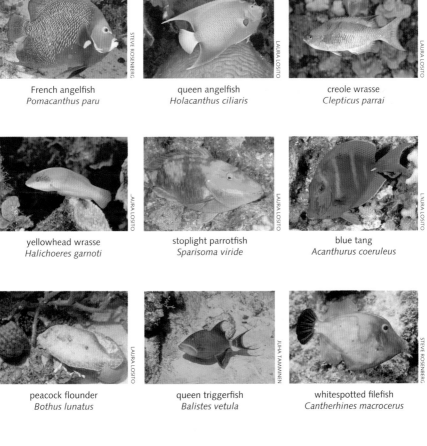

yellowhead wrasse
*Halichoeres garnoti*

stoplight parrotfish
*Sparisoma viride*

blue tang
*Acanthurus coeruleus*

peacock flounder
*Bothus lunatus*

queen triggerfish
*Balistes vetula*

whitespotted filefish
*Cantherhines macrocerus*

spotted trunkfish
*Lactophrys bicaudalis*

sharpnose puffer
*Canthigaster rostrata*

bridled burrfish
Cyclichthys antennatus

## Common Invertebrates

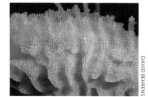
azure vase sponge
*Callyspongia plicifera*

variable boring sponge
*Siphonodictyon coralliphagum*

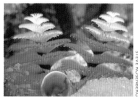
Christmas tree worm
*Spirobranchus giganteus*

Caribbean reef octopus
*Octopus briareus*

Caribbean reef squid
*Sepioteuthis sepioidea*

Caribbean spiny lobster
*Panulirus argus*

sculptured slipper lobster
*Parribacus antarcticus*

channel clinging crab
*Mithrax spinosissimus*

cushion sea star
*Oreaster reticulatus*

ruby brittle star
*Ophioderma rubicundum*

giant basket star
*Astrophyton muricatum*

blue bell tunicates
*Clavelina puertosecensis*

# Hazardous Marine Life

Marine animals almost never attack divers, but many have defensive and offensive weaponry that can be triggered if they feel threatened or annoyed. The ability to recognize hazardous creatures is a valuable asset in avoiding injury. Following are some of the potentially hazardous creatures most commonly found in the Bay Islands.

## Shark

Sharks come in many shapes and sizes. They are most recognizable by their triangular dorsal fin. Though many species are shy, there are occasional attacks. About 25 species worldwide are considered dangerous to humans. Sharks will generally not attack unless provoked, so don't taunt, tease or feed them. Avoid spearfishing, carrying fish baits or

STEVE ROSENBERG

mimicking a wounded fish, and your likelihood of being attacked will greatly diminish. Face and quietly watch any shark that is acting aggressively and be prepared to push it away with a camera, knife or tank. If someone is bitten by a shark, stop the bleeding, reassure the patient, treat for shock and seek immediate medical aid.

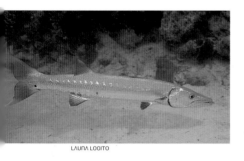

LAURA LOOITO

## Barracuda

Barracuda are identifiable by their long, silver, cylindrical bodies and razorlike teeth protruding from an underslung jaw. They swim alone or in small groups, continually opening and closing their mouths, an action that looks daunting but actually assists their respiration. Though barracuda will hover near divers to observe, they are really somewhat shy, though they may be attracted by shiny objects that resemble fishing lures. Irrigate a barracuda bite with fresh water and treat with antiseptics, anti-tetanus and antibiotics.

## Scorpionfish

Scorpionfish are well-camouflaged creatures that have poisonous spines along their dorsal fins. They are often difficult to spot since they typically rest quietly on the bottom or on coral, looking more like rocks. Practice good buoyancy control and watch where you put your hands. Scorpionfish wounds can be excruciating. To treat a puncture, wash the wound and immerse it in nonscalding hot water for 30 to 90 minutes.

DAVID BEHRENS

**121**

DAVID BEHRENS

## Moray Eel

Distinguished by their long, thick, snakelike bodies and tapered heads, moray eels come in a variety of colors and patterns. Don't feed them or put your hand in a dark hole—eels have the unfortunate combination of sharp teeth and poor eyesight, and will bite if they feel threatened. If you are bitten, don't try to pull your hand away suddenly—the teeth slant backward and are extraordinarily sharp. Let the eel release it and then surface slowly. Treat with antiseptics, anti-tetanus and antibiotics.

## Stingray

Identified by its diamond-shaped body and wide "wings," the stingray has one or two venomous spines at the base of its tail. Stingrays like shallow waters and tend to rest on silty or sandy bottoms, often burying themselves in the sand. Often only the eyes, gill slits and tail are visible. These creatures are harmless unless you sit or step on them. Though injuries are uncommon, wounds are always extremely painful, and often deep and infective. Immerse wound in nonscalding hot water and seek medical aid.

STEVE ROSENBERG

## Fire Worm

Also called bristle worms, fire worms are found on most reefs. They have segmented bodies covered with either tufts or bundles of sensory hairs that extend in tiny, sharp, detachable bristles. If you touch one, the tiny stinging bristles lodge in your skin and cause a burning sensation that may be followed by a red spot or welt. Remove embedded bristles with adhesive tape, rubber cement or a commercial facial peel. Apply a decontaminant such as vinegar, rubbing alcohol or dilute ammonia.

DAVID BEHRENS

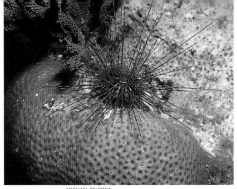

MICHAEL BEHRENS

## Sea Urchin

Sea urchins tend to live in shallow areas near shore and come out of their shelters at night. They vary in coloration and size, with spines ranging from short and blunt to long and needle-sharp. The spines are the urchin's most dangerous weapon, easily able to penetrate neoprene wetsuits, booties and gloves. Treat minor punctures by extracting the spines and immersing the area in nonscalding hot water. More serious injuries require medical attention.

## Fire Coral

DAVID BEHRENS

Although often mistaken for stony coral, fire coral is a hydroid colony that secretes a hard, calcareous skeleton. Fire coral grows in many different shapes, often encrusting or taking the form of a variety of reef structures. It is usually identifiable by its tan, mustard or brown color and finger-like columns with whitish tips. The entire colony is covered by tiny pores and fine, hairlike projections nearly invisible to the unaided eye. Fire coral "stings" by discharging small, specialized cells called nematocysts. Contact causes a burning sensation that lasts for several minutes and may produce red welts on the skin. Do not rub the area, as you will only spread the stinging particles. Cortisone cream can reduce the inflammation, and antihistamine cream is good for killing the pain. Serious stings should be treated by a doctor.

## Touch-Me-Not Sponge

They may be beautiful, but sponges can pack a powerful punch with fine spicules that sting on contact, even after they've washed up on shore. Red sponges often carry the most potent sting, although they are not the only culprits. If you touch a stinging sponge, do not rub the area. Remove visible spicules with tweezers, adhesive tape, rubber cement or a commercial facial peel. Soak in vinegar for 10 to 15 minutes. The pain usually goes away within a day. Cortisone cream can help.

DAVID BEHRENS

# Diving Conservation & Awareness

DAVID BEHRENS

Marine ecologists recognize the Bay Islands' fringing reefs and sheer drop-offs as some of the most diverse and healthy in the Caribbean. That hasn't always been the case, however. Years ago lobsters, conchs and groupers were being overfished, and poor anchoring practices and runoff from shoreline development had damaged the reefs.

Today moorings mark all dive sites, several retired vessels have been sunk to create artificial reefs, officials patrol the marine reserves, and local and international efforts are underway to study and preserve this productive and dynamic marine ecosystem.

## Marine Reserves & Regulations

Established on Roatán in the late 1980s, the Sandy Bay–West End Marine Reserve stretches for seven miles, from the east side of Sandy Bay past West End village and West Bay to the southern side of West End Point. Dive operators maintain a series of moorings in the reserve, and commercial fishing, lobstering and conch harvesting are prohibited. As a result, the corals are thriving, and fish and invertebrates are plentiful. Divers and snorkelers who visit as part of a dive resort package are charged US$10 each to help with the reserve's efforts.

Guanaja has been designated a marine reserve from the mean high-tide mark to a depth of nearly 200ft (60m). Visitors are prohibited from anchoring, discharging bilge water or sewage, standing on or damaging coral, or fishing by spear, net, trap or hook and line. It's also illegal to harvest, collect or sell coral, sponges, shells, conchs, lobsters, turtles, iguanas or green parrots.

A sensitive turtle-nesting habitat, Utila's Turtle Harbour is closed to fishing, lobstering and conch harvesting. Off the island's west end, Ragged Cay is a protected rookery for frigate birds and pelicans.

The largest research effort to date was centered on the Cayos Cochinos, where the Smithsonian Tropical Research Institute conducted a number of field studies in the mid-1990s. Today the entire Cayos Cochinos island group is a protected biological marine reserve. Boats must use established moorings (anchoring is not allowed), and commercial fishing is forbidden.

# Responsible Diving

Dive sites are often along reefs and walls covered in beautiful corals and sponges. It only takes a moment—an inadvertently placed hand or knee, or a careless brush or kick with a fin—to destroy this fragile, living part of our delicate ecosystem. By following certain basic guidelines while diving, you can help preserve the ecology and beauty of the reefs:

1. Never drop boat anchors onto a coral reef and take care not to ground boats on coral. Encourage dive operators and regulatory bodies in their efforts to establish permanent moorings at appropriate dive sites.

2. Practice and maintain proper buoyancy control and avoid overweighting. Be aware that buoyancy can change over the period of an extended trip. Initially you may breathe harder and need more weighting; a few days later you may breathe more easily and need less weight. Tip: Use your weight belt and tank position to maintain a horizontal position—raise them to elevate your feet, lower them to elevate your upper body. Also be careful about buoyancy loss: As you go deeper, your wetsuit compresses, as does the air in your BC.

3. Avoid touching living marine organisms with your body and equipment. Coral polyps can be damaged by even the gentlest contact. Never stand on or touch living coral. The use of gloves is no longer recommended: Gloves make it too easy to hold on to the reef. The abrasion caused by gloves may be even more damaging to the reef than your hands. If you must hold on to the reef, touch only exposed rock or dead coral.

4. Take great care in underwater caves. Spend as little time within them as possible, as your air bubbles can damage fragile organisms. Divers should take turns inspecting the interiors of small caves and beneath ledges to lessen the chances of damaging contact.

5. Be conscious of your fins. Even without contact, the surge from heavy fin strokes near the reef can do damage. Avoid full-leg kicks when diving close to the bottom and when leaving a photo scene. When you inadvertently

Resist the urge to chase or otherwise harass turtles.

DAVID BEHRENS

kick something, stop kicking! It seems obvious, but some divers either panic or are totally oblivious when they bump something. When treading water in shallow reef areas, take care not to kick up clouds of sand. Settling sand can smother the delicate reef organisms.

6. Secure gauges, computer consoles and the octopus regulator so they're not dangling—they are like miniature wrecking balls to a reef.

7. When swimming in strong currents, be extra careful about leg kicks and handholds.

8. Photographers should take extra precautions, as cameras and equipment affect buoyancy. Changing f-stops, framing a subject and maintaining position for a photo often conspire to thwart the ideal "no-touch" approach on a reef. When you must use "holdfasts," choose them intelligently (e.g., use one finger only for leverage off an area of dead coral).

9. Resist the temptation to collect or buy coral or shells. Aside from the ecological damage, collection of marine souvenirs depletes the beauty of a site and spoils other divers' enjoyment. The same goes for marine archaeological sites (mainly shipwrecks). Respect their integrity. Some sites are even protected from looting by law.

10. Ensure that you take home all your trash and any litter you may find as well. Plastics in particular pose a serious threat to marine life.

11. Resist the temptation to feed fish. You may disturb their normal eating habits, encourage aggressive behavior or feed them food that is detrimental to their health.

12. Minimize your disturbance of marine animals. Don't ride on the backs of turtles or manta rays, as this can cause them great anxiety.

## Marine Conservation Organizations

Coral reefs and oceans face unprecedented environmental pressures. The following groups are actively involved in promoting responsible diving practices, publicizing environmental marine threats and lobbying for better policies:

**CORAL: The Coral Reef Alliance**
☎ 510-848-0110
www.coralreefalliance.org

**Cousteau Society**
☎ 757-523-9335
www.cousteausociety.org

**Project AWARE Foundation**
☎ 949-858-7657
www.padi.com/aware

**ReefKeeper International**
☎ 305-358-4600
www.reefkeeper.org

**Smithsonian Tropical Research Institute**
☎ 507-212-8000
www.stri.org

**Reef Environmental Education Foundation**
☎ 305-451-0312
www.reef.org

**Reef Relief**
☎ 305-294-3100
www.reefrelief.org

# Listings

## Telephone Calls

To call the Bay Islands, dial the international access code for the country you are calling from (in the U.S. it's 011) + 504 (Honduras' country code) + the 7-digit local number. Many of the phone numbers below are the U.S.-based booking offices. Toll-free numbers (800, 877 or 888) can be accessed from the U.S. and, usually, Canada.

## Diving Services

Following is a list of reliable, well-established dive operators and resorts. The resorts all have in-house dive shops and provide package deals. Most of the operations listed offer certification and advanced and specialty diving courses. Most shops also rent or sell brand-name scuba gear and accept major credit cards. Many offer special trips, including snorkeling, fishing, kayaking and other tours. A few shops offer instruction in a range of languages—German, Italian, Dutch, etc.

### Roatán

**Anthony's Key Resort**
Sandy Bay
toll-free ☎ 800-227-3483
☎ 954-929-0090
fax: 954-922-7478 (U.S.)
www.anthonys-key.com
akr@anthonyskey.com

**Bananarama Dive Center**
West End Village
☎ 992-9679  fax: 445-1394
www.roatanet.com/bananarama
bananarama@globalnet.hn

**Bay Islands Beach Resort**
Sandy Bay
toll-free ☎ 800-476-2826
☎ 561-624-5774
fax: 561-624-7751 (U.S.)
www.bibr.com
bibrusa@aol.com

**CoCo View Resort**
French Harbour
toll-free ☎ 800-282-8932
☎ 352-588-4132
fax: 352-588-4158 (U.S.)
☎ 455-5011  fax: 455-5013
www.cocoviewresort.com
ccv@roatan.com

**Coral Gardens Resort**
West End Village
toll-free ☎ 877-863-4834
☎ 318-217-0691 (U.S.)
☎ 445-1428
www.coralgardensresort.com
info@coralgardensresort.com

## Roatán (continued)

### Fantasy Island Beach Resort
French Harbour
toll-free ☎ 800-282-8932
or 800-676-2826
fax: 352-588-4158 (U.S.)
☎ 455-5222/5191
fax: 455-5268/5287
www.fantasyislandresort.com
fantasy@bonnebeach.com

### Inn of the Last Resort
Sandy Harbour
toll-free ☎ 888-238-8266
☎ 445-1838/1902/1903
fax: 445-1848
www.innoflastresort.com
information@innofthelastresort.net

### Keifito's Plantation
West End Village
www.caribbeancoast.com/nhotels/
keifitosplantation
keifitosplantation@worldvacations.com

### Oak Bay Resort
Oak Ridge
toll-free ☎ 800-493-8426
☎ 504-435-2337
www.roatandiving.com
ahopn@arrl.net

### Ocean Divers
West End Village
www.oceandivers.net
oceandivers@global.hn

### Paya Bay Resort
East End
toll-free ☎ 877-509-7823
☎ 936-628-2204
fax: 936-628-3554 (U.S.)
☎ 435-2139/2172  fax: 435-2149
www.payabay.com/frames.htm
payabay-usa@mindspring.com

### Reef House Resort
Oak Ridge
toll-free ☎ 800-328-8897
☎ 210-681-2888
fax: 210-733-7889 (U.S.)
☎ 435-2297
www.reefhouseresort.com
reefdiving@aol.com

### Puravida Resort
West End Village
☎ 445-1141 phone/fax
www.puravidaresort.com
puravida@hondutel.hn

### Roatán's Dive & Yacht Club
French Harbour
toll-free ☎ 800-282-8932
☎ 445-5233  fax: 455-5407
www.roatanyachtclub.com
mh@roatanyachtclub.com

### Sueño del Mar Dive Center
West End Village
toll-free ☎ 800-298-9009
☎/fax  445-1717
www.suenodelmar.com
suenodelmar@globalnet.hn

### Sunnyside Vista Villa
Sandy Bay
☎ 202-342-0191 (U.S.)
☎/fax  445-1498
roatan-island.awwm.com
vistarent@aol.com

### West End Divers
West End Village
☎ 445-1531
www.roatanet.com/wed
paradise@globalnet.hn

### West Bay Village
Coxen Hole
☎/fax: 995-4468
www.westbayvillage.com
lascupulas@earthlink.net

# Barbareta

**Barbareta Beach Resort**
toll-free ☎ 888-450-3483
☎ 208-756-2799
fax: 208-756-8246 (U.S.)
barbareta@wildernessriver.com

# Guanaja

**Bayman Bay Club**
toll-free ☎ 800-524-1823
☎ 954-472-3700
fax: 954-723-0044 (U.S.)
www.baymanbayclub.com
info@baymanbayclub.com

**Dunbar Rock Villa**
Bonacca
toll-free ☎ 800-535-7063
fax: 830-598-4328
☎ 453-4506
www.bayislandsdirectory.com/crystal
crystalbeachresorts@tstar.net

**End of the World Resort**
Michael's Rock
☎ 991-1257
www.guanaja.com
endoftheworld@compuserve.com

**Nautilus Dive Resort**
Sandy bay
toll-free ☎ 800-535-7063
☎ 453-4389
Fax: 800-598-4328 (U.S.)
www.bayislandsdirectory.com/nautilus/
crystalbeachresorts@tstar.net

**Posada del Sol**
toll-free ☎ 800-282-8932
☎ 352-588-4132
fax: 352-588-4158 (U.S.)
www.posadadelsol.com
info@posadadelsol.com

# Cayos Cochinos

**Plantation Beach Resort**
☎ 442-0974
www.plantationbeachresort.com
pbr@laceiba.com

# Utila

**Bay Islands College of Diving**
El Centro
☎ 504-425-3143
www.dive-utila.com
bicdive@hondutel.hn

**Cross-Creek Dive Center**
El Centro
☎ 425-3134/3334  fax: 425-3234
www.ccreek.com
scooper@hondutel.hn

## Utila (continued)

### Ecomarine Gunter's Dive Shop
Sandy Bay
☎ 504-425-3350
fax: 504-425-3305
ecomar@hondutel.hn

### Laguna Beach Resort
toll-free ☎ 800-668-8452
☎ 337-893-0013
fax: 337-893-5024 (U.S.)
www.utila.com
res@utila.com

### Paradise Divers
El Centro
☎ 504-425-3148
fax: 504-425-3348
paradisedivers@yahoo.com

### Parrot's Dive Center
El Centro
☎ 425-3159
www.parrots-dive-center.com
info@parrots-dive-center.com

### Utila Lodge
El Centro
toll-free ☎ 800-282-8932
☎ 352-588-4132
fax: 352-588-4158 (U.S.)
www.roatan.com/utilalodge
utl@roatan.com

### Utila Dive Centre
El Centro
☎ 425-3326  fax: 425-3327
www.utiladivecentre.com
info@utiladivecentre.com

# Live-Aboard

### Bay Islands Aggressor IV
Aggressor Fleet Ltd.
☎ 985-384-0817
fax: 985-384-0817 (U.S.)
toll-free ☎ 800-348-2628
www.aggressor.com
info@aggressor.com
**Home port:** Dock at Parrot Tree Plantation Resort, Roatán
**Description:** 120ft aluminum monohull
**Accommodations:** 8 queen staterooms, 2 king staterooms
**Passenger capacity:** 20
**Destinations:** All major island groups
**Duration:** 7 days

# Index

dive sites covered in this book appear in **bold** type

# Lonely Planet Pisces Books

The **Diving & Snorkeling** guides cover top destinations worldwide. Beautifully illustrated with full-color photos throughout, the series explores the best diving and snorkeling areas and prepares divers for what to expect when they get there. Each site is described in detail, with information on suggested ability levels, depth, visibility and, of course, marine life. There's basic topside information as well for each destination.

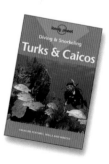

## Also check out dive guides to:

Australia's Great Barrier Reef

Australia: Southeast Coast

Bali & Lombok

Bermuda

Bonaire

Chuuk Lagoon, Pohnpei & Kosrae

Cocos Island

Curaçao

Dominica

Fiji

Guam & Yap

Jamaica

Maldives

Monterey Peninsula & Northern California

Pacific Northwest

Philippines

Puerto Rico

Red Sea

Scotland

Seychelles

Southern California & the Channel Islands

Tahiti & French Polynesia

Thailand

Texas

Vanuatu

# Lonely Planet

| | |
|---|---|
| **travel guidebooks** | in-depth coverage with background and recommendations |
| **shoestring guides** | for those with plenty of time and limited money |
| **condensed guides** | highlight the best a destination has to offer |
| **citySync** | digital city guides for Palm™ OS |
| **outdoor guides** | walking, cycling, diving and watching wildlife series |
| **phrasebooks** | including unusual languages and two-way dictionaries |
| **city maps and road atlases** | essential navigation tools |
| **world food** | explores local cuisine and produce |
| **out to eat** | a city's best places to eat and drink |
| **read this first** | invaluable pre-departure guides |
| **healthy travel** | practical advice for staying well on the road |
| **journeys** | great reading for armchair explorers |
| **pictorial** | lavishly illustrated coffee table books |
| **ekno** | low-cost phonecard with e-services |
| **website** | for chat, upgrades, and up-to-date destination facts |
| **lonely planet images** | online photo library |

## Download free guidebook upgrades at:

### *www.lonelyplanet.com*

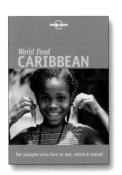

# Lonely Planet Offices

**Australia**
Locked Bag 1, Footscray, Victoria 3011
☎ 03 8379 8000  fax 03 8379 8111
talk2us@lonelyplanet.com.au

**UK**
10a Spring Place, London NW5 3BH
☎ 020 7428 4800 fax 020 7428 4828
go@lonelyplanet.co.uk

**USA**
150 Linden Street, Oakland, CA 94607
☎ 510 893 8555, or 800 275 8555 (toll free)
fax 510 893 8572
info@lonelyplanet.com

**France**
1 rue du Dahomey, 75011 Paris
☎ 01 55 25 33 00 fax 01 55 25 33 01
bip@lonelyplanet.fr
www.lonelyplanet.fr

**World Wide Web: www.lonelyplanet.com *or* AOL keyword: lp**
**Lonely Planet Images: www.lonelyplanetimages.com**